Classroom
Talk

Edited by David Booth and Carol Thornley-Hall

HEINEMANN
Portsmouth, NH

For all the teachers who
participated in the Peel TALK Project.

© 1991 Pembroke Publishers Limited
528 Hood Road
Markham, Ontario
L3R 3K9

Published in the U.S.A. by
Heinemann Educational Books, Inc.
361 Hanover Street
Portsmouth, NH 03801-3959
ISBN (U.S.) 0-435-08596-4

Canadian Cataloguing in Publication Data

Main entry under title:

Classroom talk

ISBN 0-921217-65-X

1. Oral communication. 2. Communication in
education. I. Booth, David W. (David Wallace),
1938- . II. Thornley-Hall, Carol, 1936- .

LB1572.T35 1991   371.1'022   C91-094040-1

Editor: David Kilgour
Design: John Zehethofer
Typesetting: Jay Tee Graphics Ltd.

Printed and bound in Canada
9 8 7 6 3 4 2 1

Contents

Introduction 5

1. **Talking to Learn: Interactive Learning as a Classroom Model** 7

    Types of Problem-Solving Talk in the Classroom 9
        by Susan Huff
    Peer Leaders in Group Discussion 17
        by Christine Collis
    Talk and the Quiet Child 24
        by Barbara Knapp

2. **Enhancing Literacy through Talk: Relating Text and Talk** 30

    Moving into Literacy through Reading Aloud in Junior
        Kindergarten 31
        by Gail Pillman
    Responding to Books as a Family 41
        by Donna Nesbitt
    Classroom Story Talk: The Challenges Facing the
        Teacher 45
        by Jane Thomson
    Talk and Peer Conferencing in the Writing Process 49
        by Anne Krant

3. **Talk across the Curriculum: Talk as a Way of Learning in Every Subject** 59

    Talking and Cooperating 60
        by Debbie Gibson, Lori Mattartollo, Jim Vincent
    Talk and Computers 67
        by John Forth and Catherine Morrison
    Positive Talk to Promote Self-Esteem and Learning 68
        by Nancy Turner
    Current Events as a Springboard for Talk and
        Drama 75
        by Beverley Philips

4. Drama as a Way of Learning: The Role of Talk in Dramatic Activity *84*

Storytelling with Junior Kindergarten Children *85*
    by Carolyn Davis
Dramatic Play in Grade One *87*
    by Evelyn Bruno

5. Talk and the ESL Child *93*

The Role of Personality in the Acquisition of a Second
    Language *94*
        by Shelley Katz
Communication through Body Talk *99*
        by Ruth Ichiyen
Talk between Buddies *102*
        by Kathleen Lewis

Epilogue: Reflections on the Talk Curriculum *105*
                by Dave Riddell

Bibliography *115*

Introduction

In 1988, the Ontario Ministry of Education and the Peel Board of Education established a three-year project to explore talk within the context of classroom learning. It seemed to those of us who organized the project that talk is a vital component of learning in every area of the curriculum, that its benefits had not been scrutinized by teachers in a practical way, for the simple reason that they hadn't been given the opportunity. The TALK Project was designed to support teachers as they began to examine their own classroom practice by observing their students in action and then analysing and reflecting upon their observations in order to change their teaching.

Over the course of the first year of the project, the project consultants, Carol Thornley-Hall, David Booth, Gordon Wells, Gen Ling Chang, Sar Khan, and Barbara Knapp, met with teachers in various contexts — at conferences with individual teachers, in school meetings, during catalyst committee meetings, at Ministry courses, and in principal seminars. No strict guidelines were set down: each teacher was free to explore whatever facet of talk interested him or her. This proved to be the most difficult of all our tasks, for the balance of encouraging independent growth while encouraging and enabling participation by as many teachers as possible was difficult to maintain.

Teachers from eight schools took part in the project in a variety of ways, from the private reading of resources supplied by the consultants, to the public sharing of classroom research. The schools were given access to audio and video equipment, and some brief training sessions were offered to volunteers. Over three years, eighty teachers were committed to classroom-based research projects, and this book is a compilation of many of the papers that were received from the participants. You will find that they reflect the individual interests, styles, and experiences of the teachers: some are formal in tone, others informal; some use scientific research models, others are highly personal. We encouraged this diversity by refusing to establish predetermined standards about subjects, treatments, etc. Although we tried to offer support when it was needed, we also tried to give the teachers free rein — much the same as many of them were trying to give their own students — in the hope that they would pursue interests that would make a real difference to them and to their students.

There were too many papers to be included in one book: some were written on similar topics and others were works in progress; some were written specifically for a particular program, while others were personal narratives. The papers that were selected for this book represent the various types of exploration the teachers were engaged in, and in some ways, connect the reader to outcomes of the Peel TALK Project. (Some papers that have not been included are summarized in the introductions to the chapters.)

This book, then, is very much "a report from the front". Its companion volume, *The Talk Curriculum*, contains the theoretical writings that acted as a framework for these teacher investigations and influenced many of us involved in the project. What the papers in this volume demonstrate is the extraordinary enthusiasm, intelligence, and originality that teachers can bring to classroom research. None of these papers attempts to be definitive or conclusive, but they all reveal the enormous range of possibilities teachers can explore on their own or as part of collaborative teams, with or without the help of consultants and elaborate equipment. Like the people who wrote them — and the students they teach — these articles represent forces and ideas in a period of great change and challenge in education, teachers helping each other to become more professional in their dealings with children; teachers becoming responsible for the effectiveness of their own programs; teachers talking with each other, with children, and with educators concerned with talk in the classroom.

What has struck us most about this work is the constantly recurring statement that what matters most at this crucial time is the need for us to *listen*, not only to experts and to our own instincts, but, first and foremost, to the children with whom we spend our working lives.

David Booth
Carol Thornley-Hall

1. Talking to Learn: Interactive Learning as a Classroom Model

Perhaps it is because we take "talk" for granted that it has received such little attention in the school day. But as adults, we use this medium to think aloud, to tentatively explore the beginnings of ideas, to "hitchhike" on what others have said, to clarify and modify our knowledge base, to affirm the thoughts of others, to acknowledge and enable speakers to continue groping for meaning. However, children traditionally have been rewarded for using talk in a much more structured, formal way, often only in a question-and-answer pattern, where hesitation and change are not rewarded. To observe children engaged in activities that require conversation is to understand the nature of learning, and teachers are attempting to discover how talk can promote thought and language development in interactive situations. The following papers focus on classroom talk as a model for intellectual and emotional growth, but there were many other good studies that could not be included here.

Lynn Campbell's study, for instance, examined the physical arrangement of her Grade Two classroom: how do parallel or cooperative groupings affect the ratio of "social" or "on-task" talk in the classroom? In a cooperative grouping the children were organized in groups of three using their individual desks as working surfaces, with materials and equipment limited to one of everything, so that sharing was necessary. In a parallel activity, the work surface remained the same but students each had their own set of materials and equipment. To simplify the observation and transcribing process, Lynn limited the inquiry to three students. The principal assisted in videotaping the inquiry group, while Lynn audiotaped the sessions. She concluded, after several weeks, that the cooperative activities involved a greater percentage of "on-task" talk than the parallel sessions. The results of Lynn's enquiry supported the use of cooperative activity as an effective learning tool in the classroom.

In her journal, Dianna Hector compiled her reflections on counseling students in her role as vice-principal. After audio-taping sessions, she began to assess and study her own counseling techniques. Dianna found that a guidance counselor needs to take time with children, to discuss their worries, to ease anxieties and shift to positive approaches in solving their problems, to help them redirect their hostilities into more positive responses. Her goal is to help children to progress to a sense of mastery and healthy self-esteem. Dianna changed her teaching approach by reflecting on the talk that grew from one-on-one situations in her interactions with children in difficulty.

During meetings of an in-school review committee, Lydia Renahan, working in a consultative role in special education, noted difficulties encountered with the behavior of junior-aged students at the school. Teachers were identifying individual students as demonstrating physical aggression, restlessness, inattention, and other disruptive behavior in the classroom. The resource team asked her to coordinate the organization of a social skills group, involving eight students in difficulty. Lydia organized a non-elected student council composed of the eight students along with five students considered "socially appropriate" by teachers and peers. The purpose of her inquiry was to determine if direct teaching of social talk would help the students in difficulty. A program of communication lab activities was begun, using the sharing of books containing problems in social interaction, followed by problem-solving discussions. Each time, one person acted as an observer who reported back to the group after each session. The results were positive, and the teachers noticed social growth in the eight students. Lydia had facilitated the discovery of the power of appropriate talk during the group meetings, and had provided the students with the opportunity to relate to peers in a positive way.

In Margaret Telford's classroom, there is a photograph album in the book corner available to children and visitors as part of her regular publications program. The pictures in the album were taken by the teacher or submitted by parents. By audio/videotaping children with the album, Margaret was able to observe and note the language of the children as they sorted the pictures, sequenced events, counted boys and girls in the photos, etc. The tapes demonstrated the quality of talk that emerged, especially from quiet children and ESL students. The albums stimulated the children to respond through discussion.

Mary Bayne joined a group of six children on the "story carpet" in her Grade One classroom and videotaped them in storying sessions in which one child would begin a story, perhaps from a teacher-written story starter activity card, and other children would then add to and continue the narrative. The children would tell each other if a new piece did not fit, and during the year the stories became longer and more polished. As well, their group storying experience appeared to assist them in their peer-conferencing about their own written compositions. The enthusiasm of the children for the project continued to the end of the school year.

The three papers that follow show the sort of insights that can result from careful observation of talk in the classroom.

Types of Problem-Solving Talk in the Classroom
SUSAN HUFF

The TALK Project interested me from the start, but I felt that with only one year of teaching experience, I might not be able to participate. But after meeting some of the people involved and watching them in action, I was convinced that I should become part of it.

My involvement began in mid-January. The proposal that I developed was designed to investigate "types of talk and how children use talk to solve problems". My aim was to help children become "self-directed, self-motivated, independent problem-solvers" — just as the Ontario Ministry of Education urges. I began to collect data (written and audiotaped) as children were working out their own problems — spontaneously, as they occurred. As time went on I realized that the tape machine was not always accessible when these "problems" occurred. It was suggested that I prepare and present a problem to the children; this way, I would be prepared to record their responses with video machines or in writing.

The children were divided into three groups, so that student talk could be heard. The groups were made up on the basis of their verbal input during large group gatherings such as "our time together" (opening exercises in the morning). It was fairly easy to establish these groups as some children very freely and willingly contributed and others said next to nothing day after day. The groups became: verbal (nine children); non-verbal (eight children); and mixed (nine children).

A prepared problem would be presented to one group at a time. While this group was working on the problem, the other two groups carried on with their daily activities. When the group agreed on a solution or simply solved the problem, the videotaping would end and the groups would rotate. Materials would be arranged so that the next group could begin the same way. Three problems were presented to each group and recorded on video. The result was nine "cells" of videotaped data.

Throughout the duration of my involvement in the project, audio and written recordings were made as well, but the above-mentioned cells of video material became the focus of my attention.

The problems were as follows:

Problem #1
Try to balance a marble on a plank of wood supported by four uneven posts. You may find other things in the classroom to help if you think more materials will assist you.
Materials: 1 plank of wood 7" × 10" × 1"
4 uneven posts 6", 6½", 7", 6¾"
1 marble
Children ended up using lego, plasticine, and pattern blocks to shim up the uneven posts.

Problem #2
Try to place 75 various sized lids and caps into a small basket. At the end you must be able to lift the basket.
Materials: 75 various sized lids and caps
1 plastic storage basket 8" × 5" × 3"
None of the groups were able to fit all of the lids into the basket. Therefore the challenge became, "How few lids can you leave out?" The fewer the better. Groups compared numbers.

Problem #3
Build a free-standing tower with a 15-minute time limit.
Materials: 2 pieces of 6" × 8" bristol board
10 paperclips
1 pair of scissors
All groups were able to make their structure stand by cutting

10

the bristol board and holding pieces together with paperclips.

After reviewing the tapes of the groups' attempts to solve these three problems, I found that I had over two hours of video-taped data alone. Again, I was hesitant to gather more data because I wanted to keep it simple and meaningful to me. I could see myself with eight or ten tapes and no idea how to begin making sense of it all. So I kept the research data down to a couple of audiotapes, a few pages of notes, and two full videotapes.

At this point I was thrilled with what had been recorded and pleased with the varied responses from the children. The three groups solved the problems very well. I was about to begin tran-scribing, note-making, and analysing when I realized that this part of the process could become quite overwhelming and, to say the least, frustrating. I decided to go back to my early notes for some help, and came across a talk "web" that was created in an earlier stage of the TALK Project. From then on, I made use of the web each and every time I viewed the tapes. The view-ing became fun and challenging at the same time. I was look-ing for talk examples to support the types of talk outlined in the talk web.

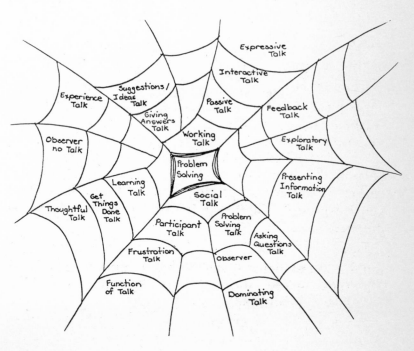

For each of the twenty-one types of talk described in the web, several examples of talk from the children could be used to support my definition. Only one or two examples were chosen as support for each.

Keeping things straightforward makes more sense to me and should make it easier for an "outsider" to understand. Rather than intimidate others who might want to try a similar study, I hope that my findings will help teachers realize what can be observed when children are talking, without being deeply committed to hours and days of taping, viewing, reading, etc.

My findings of types of talk observed were as follows:

1. *Experience Talk.* A child may use background experiences, knowledge, and previous information to add to discussion to assist in problem-solving.
   Example: Kris: "I think I know what's going on; I've built towers with my Lego stuff."

2. *Participant Talk.* Conversation from an active participant in the problem-solving situation. This talk may be directly related to the situation — topic talk — or deal with an outside experience — task talk.
   Example: Jenny: "I don't know which is better, stuffing all the little ones inside the big ones or lining them up?"

3. *Working Talk.* Giving suggestions, manipulating materials, sharing ideas, and perhaps personal background experiences.
   Example: Najme: "Well, why not try this?" [hands Emir two Lego blocks] "Maybe it'll work better."

4. *Get Things Done Talk.* An organizer who knows there is a solution or solutions acts as a motivator for the other children.
   Example: Andrew: "We know that won't work 'cause we just wasted five minutes trying. There has to be a better way."

5. *Asking Questions Talk.* Asking questions in order to gain more information which may assist in solving problems.
   Example: Flora: "Are we allowed to dump them out and try again? Want me to ask Miss Huff?"

6. *Giving Answers Talk.* Through formal answers directed

to a child who has asked a question, or based on experience, a child may provide answers or possible solutions for the situation.

Example: Vinh: "We have to make the top balance, so give me another paperclip and I'll put it on."

7. *Feedback Talk.* Responding to a question, perhaps not providing an answer but offering a comment based on discussion going on.

Example: Kate: "No! Don't do it that way! The marble has to balance on the top. No cheating."

8. *Thoughtful Talk.* Working things through, making an effort to contribute orally and solve the problem. This kind of talk may direct the other children in the right direction and arrive at a solution.

Example: Sheptim: "Guys . . . we're running out of time and we still have to do up the top. Let's just do one step at a time and not rush."

9. *Observer (No Talk).* This is the non-talk of an onlooker — this person could be interested in the subject matter but be a non-contributor because he or she has no ideas or is satisfied with the way things are being done. On the other hand, this person could have no interest whatsoever and therefore voluntarily withdraw from the group.

Example: Sieu-wei, Eva, and Cindy never talked at all.

10. *Exploratory Talk.* Could be talk about the materials, time, or other variables involved in the problem-solving situation. This talk is used to investigate possible solutions or feel things out (e.g., questions directed to the other students, troubleshooting).

Example: Chris: "I love these wooden things."
Marie: "Why don't we try stacking them — look, see how many I got into one spot!"

11. *Suggestions/Ideas Talk.* Trying to help the group out and expressing the will to contribute. Experience helps in making children feel they can vocalize their thoughts.

Example: Adriana: "Well, if you'd asked me earlier."
Kate: "We did something like this last year."

12. *Problem-solving Talk.* Active engagement in trying to solve

the problem. This kind of talk sparks interest in the task among others; it is motivating.

Example: Suzy: "We have to make it balance so why don't we try some lego, plasticine and . . . a book! to help make the posts the same size!"

Nicole: "Ya, let's get those things."

13. *Social Talk.* Children sometimes just talk about *anything* that is relevant to them — school, home, hobbies, interests, etc. This is the talk that comes from being socially involved in work or play.

Example: Adriana: "Are those Club Monaco shorts? My uncle said he would get me a pair."

14. *Frustration Talk.* Often associated with vivid facial expressions and gestures to indicate a level of frustration that can be seen as well as heard. Talk can be abrupt, with short phrases or words. Volume is usually louder than normal. Student may look for help from peers or teacher, or may give up.

Example: Jack: "Fine!" [throws down the bristol board and scissors, then moves away from the group] "You do it then, I'm not!" [sits and pouts for about six minutes]

15. *Interactive Talk.* Talk that links together conversation within the group. May be social or completely on topic.

Example: Kevin: "Try another paperclip."

Ravi: "No! That'll make it fall over."

Kevin: "Let's try it Marie's way."

16. *Learning Talk.* Children in this class have learned that the more questions you ask, the more information you gain. Learning talk may be in the form of asking questions, making observations, contributing personal experiences, or simply talking through a problem.

Example: Denise: "What will happen if we lay all the posts on their side?"

Sarah: "It looks like it'll work, maybe."

17. *Presenting Information Talk.* Noticed mainly when a "leader" or dominant participant speaks. A student may find a different way to manipulate the material to help solve the problem, and wish to share this information with the group. Troubleshooting is similar to "presenting information talk."

Example: Suzy: "The other group did it and I saw that it wasn't very tall. If we cut more pieces we'll have more paper to build with."

18. *Dominating Talk.* In any group, a leader or leaders tend to dominate the conversation at times. Usually this talk is used to suggest ideas, lend experience, show off for the camera, or actively engage in solving the problem. Some group members are turned off by this initial talk while others feel invited to contribute verbally.

Example: Adriana: "Let's everyone move back so we'll all have more room."

Andrew: "Think of the pyramids . . . they are really wide at the bottom."

19. *Passive Talk.* Quiet or unmotivated participants in the problem-solving task may display "passive" talk, which may be observed as simple short phrases, answers, or grunts. Passive participants may feel threatened by the environment or feel that the more verbal children are capable of solving the task without them. A lot of passive talk can be seen on the videos, but because these children speak more quietly and off to the side, much is not picked up by the microphone.

Example: Sherisse: "Ya." [looking on]

Cindy: [smiling and nodding]

Stephen: [to himself] "This is stupid."

Nghia: [looks at the clock]

20. *Expressive Talk.* Some children are very capable of expressing their ideas, suggestions, answers, etc. with good detail. Expressive talk is observed in children who are good readers. These children seem to be more at ease with presenting detailed information and organizing their thoughts before speaking. Often animated expressions on their faces accompany the talk.

Example: Adriana: "Getting the top to stand up straight would make the tower higher."

Andrew: "Yep! That'll do it!"

21. *Function of Talk.* Children in all three groups were able to use their oral skills to communicate with one another and try to solve the problem. Some were able to focus

directly on the task and the function of their talk was to solve the problem. Other children were able to manipulate the materials and solve the problem while discussing a topic of their own. Other children were tuning in and out of the task talk while engaging in their own topic of conversation at random. Overall, the majority of talk that was observed was related directly to the problem, its function being to solve the problem.

Conclusion

Through the use of audio and video recording, it is evident that the children used their talk to solve the problems that were presented to them. The important point is that no matter which group (verbal, non-verbal, or mixed) the children came from, when they were interested in solving the problem, the members of each group were as verbal as the next. All groups arrived at a solution in approximately the same time with very similar results.

As a result of this project, my entire program has been revised. I now plan for more opportunities for talk. This allows for and promotes cooperative learning. I now more readily accept oral presentations as a final product and place less stress on individual, written assignments. My classroom rules and expectations reflect this change in emphasis. As a teacher I see many benefits to this approach. I have developed confidence using this technique. I feel that I have grown professionally as a result of this investigation. The students have learned that their talk has value to both peers and their teacher. They are encouraged to listen to one another in a non-threatening, non-directed, and supportive environment. These experiences should extend into other social contexts.

Two years have passed since I began this inquiry and I find myself teaching several of the same children. It is apparent that they have internalized this approach; they present themselves as confident problem-solvers in both academic and general life skill situations. For example, two years ago, Jack was most frequently talking "frustration talk". Now he is perceived by his peers and teachers as a competent, cooperative group member. Other children accept him as a group leader. And *that* is a real success story!

16

Peer Leaders in Group Discussion

CHRISTINE COLLIS

My TALK project focused on the development and value of peer-initiated and peer-led meetings, and the role of peer leaders in them. It was my first year of teaching, and I was nervous, but in the end I learned a great deal.

I am convinced that the most valuable learning experiences are those which people are involved in directly and which have a meaningful link with their own lives. Prior to beginning the school year in September, I had decided that I would strive for as much student involvement in classroom design and decision-making as my Grade Three and Four students were willing to give. To facilitate this, I began regular "council meetings" which were held at least once weekly and provided an opportunity to discuss any issues which students or I felt needed to be addressed. Throughout the year, a wide variety of issues were covered. Topics included problems students were having with their studies, strategies for dealing with confrontations on the playground, input sessions for planning new units, debriefing of completed units, and making decisions about classroom routines, privileges, and the use of books and equipment.

At first, the sessions were largely teacher-directed. Students were reluctant to participate. As the class became more comfortable as a unit, the discussions became longer, and there was greater participation. I found that, although I was still initiating the meetings and many of the topics, during the discussion I spoke less frequently and the students became more involved and accustomed to voicing their own ideas.

Setting the Stage for Peer-Led Meetings

In November, the students began work on a class newspaper. They applied for jobs in five departments and, based on applications and interviews with me, the jobs were assigned. In each department, an editor assigned and oversaw the work in addition to making his or her own written contributions to the paper. A production editor managed the overall production of the paper. She met with the other five departmental editors to discuss assignments, monitor the work being completed, and help solve problems.

Videotapes of some of the meetings began to reveal to me the specific focus for my TALK project. Upon viewing the tapes I was able to see a distinct change in the conduct and productivity at meetings when an assigned editor (a peer leader) joined the discussion. The following example is characteristic of most of the meetings which took place.

Although students had already been given assignments to work on, when they met without an editor present little, if any, work was accomplished and the attention of the group drifted to unrelated topics. When the production editor sat down with the group, however, there was focused response and interest, indicated by both oral language and body position. Students were observed to actually readjust their seating, sit up straighter in their chairs, and begin to respond to the production editor's questions.

ROSEANNE (production editor): What are you doing?
NADIA: We don't know what to write about.
ROSEANNE: [making suggestions for the interview the group was to be doing] Ask things like, "Do you use a computer at home?"

In this case, Roseanne spent less than five minutes with the group, but when she left they were on task, writing down and discussing their interview questions.

Similar behavior was observed on tape involving a working meeting of the comics department. The members of this department were generally the most easily motivated of the groups, but could be distracted. They always sat together to draw and write, with their department editor working right alongside. Throughout twenty minutes of videotape, the group worked and talked. From time to time one group member or another would be distracted by another student or by interest in the video camera but would always return to work. The department editor continued working and did not leave his place. After twenty minutes, however, he finally left his seat and did not return. Within two to three minutes, the rest of the group had also left.

The tapes of these meetings suggested to me that assigned peer leaders have a great deal of influence and control over groups and are able to quickly focus group attention and keep students on track either by initiating and leading discussions or by simply being present and working alongside the group. Whenever students worked together in groups and were directed by peer editors, teacher intervention was unnecessary.

Group Meetings with Unassigned Leaders

During January, February, and March, one aspect of the math program required students to work in small groups (five to seven members), once per week, to discuss a given problem. I was usually providing input lessons to several groups during these sessions, and I was therefore often unable to observe group dynamics, relying only on the written report each group was required to submit. This was an excellent opportunity to utilize videotape.

The groups were given a problem to discuss and were asked to record possible solutions. In all cases, the groups took four to five minutes or more to focus on the question; members did not remain focused all the time. Each group submitted solutions to the problem and there were varying degrees of observed discussion. However, there was never the same amount of group discussion and decision-making as was observed during group discussions when: a) a peer leader (assigned specifically by myself or by the group) led the discussion; and b) the issue being discussed was directly related to members of the group or a relevant activity in which they were involved.

Student-initiated Meetings

While I had encouraged and set the scene for group discussions and decision-making throughout the year, it was not until early in February that the real breakthrough occurred. During a reading workshop period, two students approached me and said, "We have a problem that we would like to discuss with the rest of the class." This was it! The students explained that they felt the routine for visiting the school library was unfair and they wanted the class to talk about it. We set aside time for a class meeting that very afternoon.

I was impressed with the quantity and quality of the discussion. I realized that I probably had not been entirely fair in my most recent evaluation of the students' abilities to be independent thinkers and decision-makers. On the other hand, perhaps they had not had confidence in their own ability to take the initiative in discussions and decisions until now. The students could now claim ownership of class discussions and decisions which *they* felt were necessary.

Meeting Dynamics

During the first meeting, a particular style emerged which was further developed in subsequent meetings. Upon reflection, I realized that students were emulating some of the techniques that had been used since the beginning of the year. For example, the leader, who was always the person who had requested the meeting, ensured that everyone was given a chance to speak, if they wished, and no one could criticize a suggestion unless they were constructively modifying it. All suggestions were accepted and later evaluated and revised until a decision could be reached. During a meeting about how to decorate the classroom door for "Education Week", the group leader first opened the floor to suggestions. One suggestion after another was politely listened to but not commented on, until one student's suggestion was criticized:

DANIEL: Put a sign on the door that says school is as fun as Nintendo. [A chorus of "no", "that's dumb" from a number of students]
DANIEL: It's just an idea.
GROUP LEADER (another Daniel): Yeah. He can say what he wants to.

This unspoken rule to allow everyone the opportunity to contribute whatever they wished had been incorporated into the peer-led discussions from the first and was now being reinforced by the children on their own.

Some meeting techniques had never been introduced in the discussions which I had led and I was surprised to find them suddenly develop and become incorporated into the peer-initiated meetings. The most interesting was the final decision-making process. During the earlier meetings (led by me), we relied as much as possible on consensus and compromise in decision-making. We never resorted to an outright vote on an issue. Surprisingly, though, the concept of majority rule had somehow been instilled and *every* peer-led decision was finalized with a vote. In the discussion process, suggestions were heard from anyone who volunteered them and many ideas derived from or embellished what others had said. Through discussions, the group always narrowed its decision down to two ideas. They identified the ideas with particular student "owners" and the two students were sent from the room while the rest of the group voted.

It is interesting to note that, although the group agreed on who should leave the room, it was often necessary for the leader to clarify what one or both of the suggestions *were* before a vote could be completed. The following discussion took place during the voting process when students were deciding how to maintain a more ordered classroom library:

KATE (co-leader): Who wants to have a vote?
BESSIE (co-leader): Is that okay? Roseanne and. . .
(Unknown male voice): Brian.
BESSIE: They have to go out of the room.
   [Roseanne and Brian leave]
   [Quang starts chanting, others join in]: Brian. Brian. Brian.
LISA: What was Brian's again?
BESSIE: Does anyone remember what Brian's was? Jeffrey?
JEFFREY: Making the chart.
BESSIE: Oh yeah.
UNKNOWN: And what was Roseanne's?
BESSIE: Um. Oh yeah. Roseanne's was making the cards.
SASHA: Okay. Who wants Brian's?

This discussion is similar to all the other peer-led discussions when the group decided that it was time to vote.

All the peer-led meetings were conducted with great decorum and structure. The group sat in a circle on the carpet. The leader explained what the meeting was about and then asked for comments or suggestions. Students raised their hands and were called upon to speak by the peer leader. The rest of the group was always very quiet, polite, and intent on the issue. On many occasions, students would make reference to what another student had said previously as a preface to what they had to say. This was usually because they were either arguing a point or reconfirming and building upon an earlier suggestion. I found that these techniques and the general atmosphere and conduct at the peer-led meetings was surprisingly sophisticated.

21

I initially thought that the reason for the great decorum was that I was present in the room. I soon found, however, that students seemed to feel quite free to speak their minds when I was there and often became so involved in what they were talking about that they seemed not to notice my presence. In addition, I often made a point of leaving the room during later peer-led discussions, and when I returned a few minutes later, the group would be conducting business as usual. The only time the group became slightly disorganized was prior to voting. They quickly refocused, however, for the vote. The meetings reflected a blend of techniques which I recognized the students had learned from teacher-led discussions as well as techniques which they had developed specifically to meet their needs. Group leaders were learning by watching others and by eventually plunging in and trying things out themselves.

Student Reflections on Peer-led Meetings

At the end of the school year I was interested in discovering how the students themselves felt about student-led meetings. We met in the traditional circle and I began the meeting by reiterating the focus of my research. Briefly I explained that I had been studying what happens during meetings that are led by students. I asked them to provide their own opinions on student-led or teacher-led meetings.

The feedback was somewhat brief. Perhaps this in itself indicates more reluctance to participate in teacher-led meetings than in student-led ones. The opinions that were offered, however, were candid and very well considered. Most of those who responded felt that student-led discussions are better. Some of their responses were as follows:

> LISA: I like when kids start the meetings because then the people that are listening to that person, they get to put meetings together by themselves and sometimes when teachers do that, like, they just don't learn as much about how to put meetings together.
> BESSIE: Well, I'd rather have it led by both because, like, it's not . . . well I don't think it's fair if just the teacher led the meetings, all the meetings, or if just kids start leading all the meetings because then if just one person starts leading the meetings it's not going to be fair for the rest of the people because they

keep having to listen to what that person has to say and they don't get a chance to talk. So I'd rather have turns.

JEFFREY R.: Well, I think it's good for some people, like some students and the teacher sometimes to do it because then it gives time for the teacher to finish some of her work or something or to rest or something.

KATE: I think that it's good for the students in the classroom to lead the discussion because then if they want to be teachers when they grow up they will be ready.

ROSEANNE: I think that kids should be because lots of kids have their own ideas so if they do a meeting with just the kids and not the teacher, we can get lots of ideas. Like, say, one person says one idea then someone can say another idea. The teacher says one idea and usually we would go with that idea.

Most of the students felt that it was beneficial to their own growth to be able to learn through conducting their own meetings. They felt that it was especially important to take turns as leaders, as they recognized the value of experiential learning.

Summing Up

In conclusion, I observed growth in most of the students throughout the year as they participated in peer-led meetings. They observed and then began participating in teacher-led meetings and soon learned to take an active role in these meetings. The turning point came when students recognized their own ability to initiate and conduct group discussions. Meetings were productive and participants were fully involved when they: 1) were led by peers; 2) focused on an issue directly affecting students; and 3) were perceived by students as forums where everyone's opinion counted.

I also observed growth within myself as a first-year teacher. I had learned to put more trust in students' abilities to handle business, make decisions, and implement ideas. I also confirmed, however, that it is necessary to provide some guidance, such as setting examples for meetings. In this way students can learn strategies and modify and develop their own leadership styles and capabilities.

For me, this inquiry was a valuable tool for learning techniques in becoming an observant and reflective facilitator of learning. It is my intention to continue using class meetings in forthcoming years as an ideal forum for students to learn experientially the arts of leadership, group discussion, decision-making, refining ideas, and cooperation. I expect that each year I will become more skilled in encouraging students to take an earlier and more expanded role in the ownership of classroom business and decision-making through peer-led meetings.

Talk and the Quiet Child

BARBARA KNAPP

Whether through social talk, working talk, or rehearsed talk, when children are allowed and encouraged to express themselves verbally, they learn much more. In an environment where talk is so vitally important, where does a quiet child fit in?

This case study will attempt to describe a quiet child in his classroom environment, and to make observations on strategies that may encourage a quiet child to interact verbally and/or develop alternative methods for assimilation of new knowledge and understanding.

As research assistant on the TALK Project, I was able to observe children as I helped teachers collect data for their research. In the course of videotaping children working and learning in a variety of modes, I found I could focus on the behavior of both individuals and groups, being effectively able to exclude background noises with earphones and cut off peripheral vision with the lens of the video camera. Most often I was gathering data on children who were interacting freely and thoughtfully in a group situation.

It soon became evident to me in the microcosmic world created by the video camera that the dynamics of the group often left out certain individuals — the children who had little to say. In observing these children, I noted certain non-verbal behaviors which seemed to separate them into two groups.

First, there were children who were easily distracted, fidgeted a lot, and didn't listen to the talk which was taking place. The second group listened intently to what was going on, seemed to stay on task, but didn't interact verbally. I found that this observation concurred with research conducted by James McCroskey, who says that there are several types of quiet children ("Quiet Children in the Classroom: On Helping Not Hurting", *Communication Education*. Vol. 29: July 1980). He suggests that children may be quiet if they suffer from communication apprehension, low social self-esteem, ethnic/cultural divergence, social alienation, or skill deficiencies. Any of these factors, or a combination of these factors, may result in a quiet child.

After deciding to focus my attention on the second group, I began my study by conducting informal interviews with five children who had been identified as being quiet by two primary teachers. Surprisingly, in an informal, one-on-one situation, most of these children interacted quite openly with me as we discussed friends, school, home, and likes and dislikes. Each interview took about twenty minutes to complete, and I found that the children felt quite positive about themselves in this situation. The following responses taken from the interviews reflect some of the children's feelings about themselves in oral situations.

QUESTION: Are you a quiet person or a talkative person?
RESPONSES: [All five children thought of themselves as quiet people.]

QUESTION: Do you ever want to answer a question or share ideas, but are unable to?
RESPONSE: [All children responded yes.]

QUESTION: Why are you unable to share your ideas with the group?
RESPONSE: I get nervous and forget what I'm going to say.
Because I'm shy.
It feels not good.
I put my hand up but she doesn't pick me.
The kids don't listen to me.

QUESTION: How do you feel when others are talking and sharing their ideas?
RESPONSE: Good. I like to listen.
Mad. They won't let me in.
Sad. Because I've been asking for a long time and they say no, no. Sometimes it bothers me.
[No response.]

QUESTION: Would you rather talk or listen?
RESPONSE: [All children would rather listen.]

Although the children felt positive about themselves generally, they did feel frustrated about their lack of oral input in the classroom.

In order to put the information that I had gathered from the interviews and my case study into context, it was necessary to look at a larger body of data. I read a number of articles and studies of quiet children. Some startling facts emerged.

Thomas Conner found ("The Quiet Child: Student at Risk", *Academic Therapy*. Vol. 22, No. 5: 1987) that students' use of their verbal ability affects the form and quality of their educational experience and even influences the judgements teachers make about them. Quiet students who are less willing to talk are often underrated, misunderstood, or overlooked. And Christopher Johnson found that children who are shy do less well in various areas of academic performance ("Seen But Not Heard: The Dilemma of the Shy Child", *Momentum*. Vol. 18, No. 4: 1987).

I hoped that my own research on a quiet child would give me an opportunity to test some of these ideas.

The following description of my visit to a Grade One teacher's classroom is an attempt to see classroom events from the point of view of a quiet six-year-old boy whom I will call Jeffrey. In observing Jeffrey in a normal classroom setting, I wanted to gain some insights into the behavior of a quiet child, and understand better how to work as a teacher with such a child.

My decision to record my observation of Jeffrey by writing notes allowed me to record many non-verbal interactions that would not have been apparent on an audio tape. This method was an alternative to doing a transcription analysis, which would have been quite difficult considering the non-verbal nature of my subject.

I observed Jeffrey on six different occasions. This is a description of one of them.

As the students entered the classroom there was a quiet buzz as small conversations took place by the coat hooks, on the carpet, and around the teacher. The children observed me with only slight curiosity — I had been in their classroom on numerous occasions, videotaping small groups of children as they worked at the blocks centre. In fact, it had been during one of these videotaping sessions that I first noticed Jeffrey, the child I would be observing this morning.

On that earlier occasion, Jeffrey had chosen to be a member

26

of the group working at the blocks centre. Several of his friends were working there as well. After the play had begun they were joined by Rupert, another boy who had been drawn into the activity by his curiosity about the videocamera, and who added some wonderfully creative input to the group's building of a castle. I noticed that Jeffrey was playing by himself and not really a part of the castle group. He was certainly listening intently, however, and at one point became part of the conversation.

Rupert had suggested adding a hospital, in addition to a movie theatre, spooky graveyard, and store which had previously been suggested. Jeffrey had said nothing as these other suggestions were made, but when Rupert suggested a hospital, Jeffrey could no longer contain himself. He said, "Excuse me, but I've never heard of a hospital in a castle," in a very polite but awkward fashion. This did not fit in with any idea of a castle that he had ever heard about, and he did not seem to be able to fantasize as Rupert was doing.

On the particular morning I am about to describe, Jeffrey was near the front of the line at the school door, suggesting that he had been waiting in line before the bell rang. He came bouncing in, sporting red pants and a Nintendo T-shirt, and hung up his gym bag and sat down on the carpet in his favorite spot, the first to do so. This gave me the opportunity I needed to unobtrusively place the microphone near him. Jeffrey seemed unaffected by the microphone and even explained its presence to another boy when he asked what it was.

Erin came and sat down beside Jeffrey and a quiet conversation took place between them. The teacher, Betty, later told me that they know each other well because they both take part in the Peel Lunch and After-School Program, and are friends. Others among Jeffrey's friends were all children who could be described as quiet.

During the opening exercises, Jeffrey was listening intently. The teacher asked the children to identify words from the story on the board — Jeffrey eagerly participated, identifying several words.

It was on this question-answer period that I wanted to make some close observations. Jeffrey had been identified by his teacher as a quiet, bright child, just the person I wanted to look at in my project. How was he going to react to the teacher's questioning? He was indicating to me that he was certainly listening intently to the discussion, but would he participate? During the questioning he nodded his head in understanding, and several times his hand went up tentatively. The teacher would not have noticed that his hand was up unless she had really been looking for it.

As the class moved on to a lesson on fractions, the teacher's chart, with its brightly colored cars, boats, shoes, and bicycles, were an immediate attraction, providing the concrete examples that would be needed to assist in teaching this concept at a Grade One level. The teacher's questions seemed very clear and appropriate, but it appeared that the concept was difficult for many of the children. Four or five children attempted to answer consistently, but many were not paying attention. Jeffrey was one of those not listening — he turned around to Erin and exchanged a few words.

Betty had noticed that many of her students were not paying attention and focused on these students. And Jeffrey used a typical avoidance technique: he rolled his eyes upward so as not to make eye contact with Betty. But the knowledge that Betty was focusing on him seemed to jolt him back to paying attention. He was concentrating fully on the fraction chart, reading aloud with Betty.

Betty now asked the class to make a circle at the edge of the carpet, their normal pattern of sitting in a large group. Jeffrey was determined to reclaim his spot to the point of pushing another boy's foot out of the way to make room for himself.

In my observation of Jeffrey, I felt that I had made two important observations about him. First of all, he was not a risk-taker, which was a trait of quiet children, as I had read and observed earlier. He would only put up his hand to answer a question when he was sure he was right. As well, he was a child who needed the security of things being constant — he always chose the same place to sit in the circle (not surprisingly, this spot was with his back against the wall), and obviously thrived on the routine in Betty's class.

Both of these observations were backed up by Betty. At the same time, she offered some interesting background information about Jeffrey. There had been a great transformation in his behavior over the period of the year. At first he had really experienced difficulty in adjusting to the new expectations of Grade One and a new teacher. He had become physically sick when he was asked to do reading- or writing-related activities, or when he had to put on his snowsuit by himself. Betty felt that he had needed the extra time to become familiar with his new surroundings and expectations.

Although the focus of my observation was not on the teacher, curriculum content, or class management, I feel that it is important to note the type of atmosphere which prevailed in this particular classroom. The physical appearance of the room was similar to most Grade One classrooms that I had seen, cheerful, with colorful displays of children's work on the walls, activity centres where children could work creatively with paint, sand, or blocks, or read quietly. But it was the teacher's way of interacting with the students which I felt was most important in creating the kind of atmosphere where a quiet, uncertain child could thrive and gain confidence. Her manner seemed always to be calm, and her voice was purposefully quiet. Her students were treated with consideration and respect. Each child was allowed to be an individual, growing and developing at his or her own rate.

A teacher's leadership style affects shy children. Researchers on leadership styles have identified two distinct styles — "dominative" and "integrative" — and there are fewer socially isolated students in classrooms in which the teacher's style is integrative (i.e., more cooperative than authoritarian).

Jeffrey's teacher would most definitely fit into the second integrative category, and this may explain why Jeffrey made such positive changes over the course of the year: Betty did not ask Jeffrey to conform to what she considered normal interactive behavior, and allowed him the opportunity to grow at his own rate and develop his own way of coming into understanding. While he will probably never think aloud or often interact verbally, Jeffrey will nevertheless be able to be an integral part of the learning within any group.

This case study of Jeffrey is only a beginning. I was restricted in making my observations by limiting myself to one child, and feel that I have only touched on an area which has become very important to me, both personally and professionally. In the next stage of my study, I hope to make further observations of quiet children in a variety of situations and experiment with some methods and strategies which I feel might be effective in teaching these students.

2. Enhancing Literacy through Talk: Relating Text and Talk

Reading and writing are thought of as the primary literary activities, and yet much of our understanding of what we read comes from our discussion afterward, and preparation for writing can be greatly aided by talking over our ideas. Reading, writing, and talking are interrelated processes, and language arts activities should incorporate all three. For young children, the story being read aloud or told by the teacher comes alive through the teacher's voice. The words paint a picture in their minds, and afterwards, they can discuss their responses to the story, becoming part of the meaning-making dynamic that book talk creates. Similarly, peer conferences, where students talk to each other about their writings, blend literacy and oracy in a context for learning. Many teachers in the project found that talk and literacy do go together.

Betty-Lou Wallington and Rae Belford have been "buddying" their Grade Two and Grade Six classes for years. They felt that the occasions when the two classes got together were too short, isolated, and unrelated, and that they needed more cooperation, more interaction, and a unity of work that allowed for depth and purpose. They videotaped some sessions that grew out of a book talk with follow-up response activities. As they viewed the tapes, they became aware of how much had escaped their day-to-day observations. They had assumed that interaction always took place between the younger and the older buddies, but in reality, often the older children directed the activities and accomplished most of the tasks. Sometimes, the older children talked to each other while the younger ones sat quietly or were unable to make their points heard. They decided to show the videotapes to the older children, in order to allow them to view themselves and to reflect on their interactions. The children recognized their own need to control, and together with the teachers, the older children began to encourage more participation by the younger ones and teachers and children pooled their ideas in designing future activities.

Penny Brown saw her research inquiry as an opportunity to do some reflective thinking about a particular teaching/learning context and provide a written record of her journey. She examined the role of "thoughtful talk" in literacy and literature development, by collecting data from interviews, brainstorming sessions, workshops, and classroom recordings in order to formulate tentative conclusions for her inquiry. Using poems as a source for discussion, Penny charted the responses of the children, and through her transcripts of their talk, recognized the need for the teacher to be a facilitator and co-learner, helping the children explore possibilities, establish patterns, make connections from bits of information, and formulate plausible conclusions. Penny feels that the pursuit of analogical/ metaphorical thinking needs to be exploited in the classroom by both the teacher and the students in order for higher-level learning to take place.

The following papers show how talk can be incorporated into any language arts activity.

Moving into Literacy through Reading Aloud in Junior Kindergarten

GAIL PILLMAN

I had originally intended to begin my inquiry by looking at "Show and Tell" times and the lack of talk I've always found in these sessions. Most often, toys were brought and it became a "Bring and Brag" time. I realize that some children at four need the security of a favorite toy which will often return week after week, and I noticed this throughout the year. Adam's teddy bear, for instance, came every week in the fall term.

> ADAM: This is my teddy bear.
> TEACHER: Would you like to tell us about him?
> ADAM: I like him.
> TEACHER: Can you tell us anything else?
> ADAM: I play with him. . .

Conversations like this continued, with me asking questions and getting very short answers. Then I began to stress that books or something the children had made were my favorite "Show and Tell" things. Many more books started to appear. I made

31

a point of reading the books the children brought either to the whole class at story time or to a small group during activity time. Quite often our small groups grew to include most of the class.

At this point I decided to change my inquiry and focus on talking through the stories in books. Books were rarely chosen as an activity during playtime, and when I'd ask the children about their books they would usually tell me that they couldn't read, so they didn't know what to tell me about them. So I developed some strategies to raise the children's interest in books.

1. Teacher Reading

I read to the children every day — stories and/or poems which went along with whatever our current theme was. I also read the books that were brought in for "Show and Tell".

2. Library And Interest Centres

The children were free to take books at any time and look at them anywhere in the classroom.

3. Special Reading Spots

Two special spots were assigned just for reading. One was my rocking chair. Another was beside "Mr. Bear", a four-foot-tall stuffed bear that sat near the library centre.

4. School Library Visits

We made weekly visits to the school library, where the children heard another adult reading. They were also loaned books on a weekly basis.

5. Public Library Visits

We took monthly walking trips to our local library to hear stories, see films, and learn about public library facilities.

6. A "Snuggle Up and Read" Club

The children could sign out a book every morning upon arriving at school, take it home to read with somebody, and return it the next day. A booklet was sent home: in it parents were to record the date a book was brought home, name of the book, and who read it with the child. Each child also received a certificate stating that he/she was an official member of our club.

I had discussed this with the parents on Curriculum Night in September. When I sent home the letter outlining how our club would operate, approximately 70 percent of the parents gave permission and signed up with their children. When the parents came for interviews in early December, I discussed the club with those who had not joined. Before the Christmas break, all the children were members.

These books are from our classroom library, my own books, and books we made from photographs I took over the years and children's dictated stories to go with them.

7. Show and Tell

I encouraged the children to bring in books. As they told the stories of their books, many actually began to think of what they were doing as reading. Needless to say, they were very pleased with themselves.

8. Buddy Reading

We met with a Grade Five/Six class for a weekly half-hour session of one-on-one buddy reading. At least once a month our buddy class had to choose a book from the library or my classroom and prepare questions or a follow-up activity to go with it. The other teacher and I made sure the children asked questions that did not just require the younger children to recall detail but also made them think.

Case Studies

After implementing the above strategies, I began videotaping many children as they "read". Then I chose the following children because of their interest in books and the diversified backgrounds they brought to reading. I wanted to examine the connection between their exposure to books, their confidence and interest in looking at them, and their early reading development. The following studies track some of their experiences with particular books between February and June.

1. Marsha

Background: Marsha's verbal skills are very good. She spends a great deal of time with her grandmother, who reads to her. She has many books of her own. Marsha enjoys being the centre of attention and is very confident in all situations. She has some "writing" skills.

FEBRUARY — *VALENTINE'S DAY*, BY GAIL GIBBONS

Marsha received this book as a gift the day before she brought it for "Show and Tell". Her mother had read it to her once. She was able to recall most of it. During her reading session she was easily distracted by a problem with the back page, which kept falling out of the book.

Marsha turned the book towards her listeners to show the pictures. At the end of the story she showed the group the last page (which illustrated how to make a Valentine box) and was able to describe how to make a Valentine box in sequence.

> TEXT: Some young people wanted to choose their sweethearts by picking names from a jar.
> MARSHA: Some people . . . picking their babies by picking names from a jar.

> TEXT: Some valentines are made at home.
> MARSHA: Some valentines are made from home.

MARCH — *LITTLE RED RIDING HOOD*

Marsha made a book of this story using cut-and-paste pictures. She asked how to print the title so I printed it on a piece of paper and she copied it. By this time she was getting tired and didn't want to write anymore. She dictated her story one sentence per page. Her story matched her pictures and were in sequential order. Marsha read her book to the class.

> TEXT: P1. Little Red Riding Hood is walking on the path.
> P2. Little Red Riding Hood meets the wolf.
> P3. Little Red Riding Hood came to Grandma's house.
> P4. This is when the wolf ate up the grandma and Red Riding Hood.
> P5. The huntsman cut the wolf open. He let Grandma and Little Red Riding Hood out.
> MARSHA: P1. [Exact words]
> P2. And Little Red Riding Hood is meeting the wolf.
> P3. And Little Red Riding Hood got to Grandma's house.
> P4. And this is when — when the wolf eats Little Red Riding Hood up and Grandma.
> P5. And the huntsman came to cut the wolf open.

MAY — *LET'S LOOK AT FARMING*, BY SYLVIA PANKURST

Marsha had not seen this book before. She took it from the Interest Centre right after I had set up a display to go along with our farm unit. The text in the book was very complicated for this level. I'd chosen it because of the excellent pictures. She spent thirty-five minutes examining them.

JUNE — *MR. NOSEY*/THE *MR. MEN* SERIES, BY ROGER HARGREAVES

Marsha asked if she could read to the class. When I said yes, she went to the "Snuggle Up" shelf and picked a book, then put it on the rocker and went to play until story time. At some time over the year, she had taken this book home and read it with someone.

> TEXT: Mr. Nosey liked to know about everything that was going on. He was always poking his nose into other people's business. Mr. Nosey was the sort of a person who, if they came upon a locked door, couldn't resist looking through the keyhole to see why the door had been locked.
>
> MARSHA: Mr. Nosey was a kind old person but . . . Mr. Nosey was a nosey person. All the time he wanted to know . . . private business. There's a keyhole . . . and he tried to open up the door but it was locked.

2. Lindsay

Background: Lindsay's older brother is in a General Learning Disabilities class. Her parents are very concerned that she may have trouble in school, so they read to her a great deal. She's a very outgoing little girl and enjoys looking at books. Her articulation is very immature and often difficult to understand.

FEBRUARY — *I SEE*, BY HELEN OXENBURY

This is a pattern book with one word per page. Lindsay brought it from home and was able to read it word for word. This was the first time Lindsay read to the class. She turned the book toward her audience so they could see the pictures. Lindsay was nervous reading to the group, rocking very fast in her chair.

MARCH — *LITTLE RED RIDING HOOD*

After hearing Marsha's version of *Little Red Riding Hood*, Lindsay made her own. Her first picture was cut-and-pasted, the others were drawings. She dictated her story. When the book was completed, she waited for several days before she read it to the class. Again she was nervous and began by getting Goldilocks and Red Riding Hood mixed up.

TEXT: This is Little Red Riding Hood's house. Her mother was shopping. She had a baby-sitter.

LINDSAY: Once upon a time, there was a little girl. Her name was Goldilocks. Her mother went out shopping. She had a baby-sitter.

Throughout the rest of the story, Lindsay referred to the character as Little Red Riding Hood. In her version of the story, Lindsay had the wolf eat Grandma and Red Riding Hood before the huntsman came along, but she omitted the huntsman's rescue of the other characters, so I questioned her when she finished reading.

TEACHER: How did Grandma and Little Red Riding Hood get away from the big bad wolf?

LINDSAY: No — The big bad wolf ate Grandma up.

TEACHER: Oh. Who lived happily ever after?

LINDSAY: Grandma and the hunter and Little Red Riding Hood.

TEACHER: What did the hunter do in the story?

LINDSAY: Well, he cutted . . . first he killed him and then cutted, cut — pop! came Grandma and then Red Riding Hood.

MAY — A DINOSAUR BOOK

Lindsay made this book with cut-and-paste pictures. She took four pictures of a hatching egg and glued them in sequence in a booklet she made. She then wrote her own story using letters as symbols. When she read her book, she skipped a page.

LINDSAY: The . . . hatching the egg.
There's a hatch all around it. [referring to a crack]
At last she got out.

JUNE — HOMES, BY JAN PIENKOWSKI

Lindsay had been reading this book sitting beside "Mr. Bear". Three children joined her and she read it to them. On each page there is a picture and one word. The following page has the word "igloo" with a picture of an Eskimo climbing out of an igloo and a large polar bear standing behind it.

LINDSAY: A polar bear outside a cave.

3. Kathryn

Background: Kathryn is very interested in books. Her parents have taught her the alphabet and are trying to teach her to read at home. She's confident in discussions but gets very nervous around books.

MARCH — *BAMBI*

Kathryn made two books at home, one with stories dictated to her mother, the other with words she copied from her first story. The first one displayed left-to-right progression; the second one was made backwards. She began with the one she had made all by herself.

> KATHRYN: This is Faleen and her babies.
> This is Bambi's family.
> This is Bambi's imagination flying.

Then Kathryn showed her other book, turning the pages but saying nothing.

> TEACHER: Are you going to read the story in that one too, Kathryn?
> KATHRYN: This is [turns the book towards her and points to a word]. . .
> TEACHER: the . . .
> KATHRYN: the [turns the book towards her and points again]. . .
> TEACHER: first . . .
> KATHRYN: first [long pause] . . .
> TEACHER: Sorry, turn it around. This is the first time Bambi met. . .
> KATHRYN: Faleen? [Kathryn loses her place in the book]
> Another child: Now you don't know what page you're on.
> KATHRYN: Yes I do. [finds place]
> This is the first time Bambi met his father.
> This is Bambi's family.

APRIL

Kathryn brought a book from home. It had songs with notes and colored dots to press to play a tune. She was quite nervous and showed the book several times. I asked if she would like to play a song.

> KATHRYN: There's ten pages in here. [She finds the song "Ten Little Indians"] I know the song too.

37

TEACHER: Good.

KATHRYN: I'll sing it and I'll sing it and I'm right here, right — right — I'll just play — do it right now. [She tries to play and sing, then decides she can't do both, so sings it to the class]

JUNE — *MUD PUDDLE*, BY ROBERT MUNSCH

Kathryn chose this book to read to a small group and Mr. Bear. It is a book she also has at home and has heard many times. She appeared much more confident in this session.

TEXT: Jule Ann ran inside yelling, "Mummy, Mummy! A Mud Puddle jumped on me." Her mother took off all Jule Ann's clothes and dropped her into a big bathtub. She scrubbed Jule Ann till she was red all over.

KATHRYN: And Martha said "Mommy, Mommy a mud puddle fell on me and the dog.

TEXT: She got completely all over muddy. Even her nose was full of mud. Jule Ann ran inside yelling, "Mummy, Mummy! A Mud Puddle jumped on me."

KATHRYN: And splash everything comed on Martha.

PATRICIA: Oh my Lord!

4. Stephani

Background: Stephani is very quiet and plays by herself most of the time. At four, she is the oldest of three children and according to her mother spends her time at home making pictures. Her articulation is very immature. Her pictures are very detailed for the work of a four-year-old.

MARCH

Stephani brought two books for "Show and Tell". These were picture books with no words. The titles were "Morning" and "Night".

TEACHER: Would you like to read one of your books, Stephani?

STEPHANI: It doesn't have words in it.

TEACHER: You could read the pictures to us.

STEPHANI: Morning.

P1. It's a pretty big girl. She gots a crib.

P2. Take a shower.

P3. Look out the window.

P4. Play with her toys.

P5. Play with her friends.

Stephani made an egg-shaped book about the Easter Bunny. Her pictures were well done and her dictated sentences related to her pictures.

TEXT: Bunny was playing in the dirt.
STEPHANI: The rabbit plays in the dirt.

TEXT: Bunny was thinking about bunny monster.
STEPHANI: Bunny Rabbit thinks about a monster Bunny Rabbit.

TEXT: Bunny was delivering the Easter Eggs.
STEPHANI: Bunny Rabbit delivers the eggs.

TEXT: Bunny lives in a castle.
STEPHANI: This is Bunny Rabbit's home.

TEXT: Bunny go home.
STEPHANI: Bunny Rabbit go home.

MAY — *A DINOSAUR BOOK*

Stephani made this book with cut-and-paste pictures. She cut out and glued four pictures in correct sequence in a booklet. She began her book at the back and used letters as symbols in her writing.

STEPHANI: The egg is hatched.
     The egg is hatched all around.
     The egg [pause] had hatched.
     He's going out to play.

JUNE — *WHERE'S MOTHER?* BY ELIZABETH THORN

Stephani chose this wordless picture book to read with two peers one day. She was able to create a sequential story by reading the pictures.

5. Jaymie

Background: Jaymie was one of the last children to join the "Snuggle Up and Read Club". She often doesn't return her books for several days, saying, "My mom didn't have time to read it to me." She began to look at books in March. She has never brought a book for Show and Tell.

Jaymie began looking at books during activity time. She also began to look through the books on the "Snuggle Up" shelves, rather than take the first book she saw.

MAY — *THE HOUSE BOOK*, BY CAROL NORTH

Jaymie chose this book from the "Snuggle Up" shelves to take home. She sat down by herself to look at the book and after twenty minutes asked if she could read it to the class. She had not had it read to her.

> TEXT: Josh comes home from school. He climbs the porch steps and goes inside his house.
> JAYMIE: The little boy and the dog and the cat. And the flowers growed bigger. And — and then the dog waked up. Then the boy was going into school and he eats his lunch at school.

Results

In observing what was happening in the classroom and reviewing my tapes and anecdotal notes, I saw many positive developments:

— increased self-confidence
— developing directionally (concept of left to right, top to bottom)
— increased comprehension
— sequencing events in telling stories from texts or in writing original stories
— showing pictures and describing things in more detail
— longer attention spans
— learning to tell stories
— decision-making

Conclusions

When I sat down in April to look at my tapes, I noticed the only ones who were bringing books in and reading them were girls. The boys would bring books for "Show and Tell" but didn't read them to the group or talk about them. The first time a boy read us a book was in May. I considered adding Brian's reading to my case studies, but he just showed the pictures and answered some questions with one-word replies. I wish this weren't so, but it was the only negative thing I noticed in the period of my study.

I was pleased with the way books became a bigger part of our day. During play time, the Library Centre is now being used by some children each day. The majority of children are being read to more at home and looking at books independently.

In early June, as Leah read a book, *Pigs*, by Robert Munsch, to Marsha and Michael, this was what was heard:

LEAH: And the pig is on a stick.
MARSHA: No, it's a pole, Leah.
LEAH: Well — so — I can call it anything I want. I'm reading it.

This reinforced what I had been telling the children. "You are the reader, it's your story." I hope they have taken it to heart.

Responding to Books as a Family
DONNA NESBITT

The purpose of this inquiry was to observe the kinds of talk and modeling strategies which take place between older and younger children as they explore books together.

Our observations took place in the primary family class of Kindergarten, Grade One, and Grade Two students at Floradale Public School in Mississauga. My teaching partner, Barbara Myers, and I used audio and videotapings over the course of one year to assist us in observing the children's natural talk during our daily "Booktimes".

We both share a strong belief in the importance of giving children opportunities to explore books in a natural, comfortable environment where risk-taking is encouraged. We showed our own love of books by sharing stories, chants, poems, songs, etc., just as the more mature readers demonstrated their enjoyment of and comfort with books for the novice readers.

"Booktime" occurs twice daily for approximately fifteen to thirty minutes, depending on the children's interest. Students choose their own books to share with others or enjoy on an individual basis.

In the following transcribed excerpt from a "Booktime" conversation, two boys, Shawn, age seven, and Graeme, age six, share a picture book about the age of dinosaurs and the evolution of species, which Graeme brought from home.

41

Both boys shared a common interest in dinosaurs. Shawn was a very capable reader and was viewed as a "Dinosaur Expert" by the other children and his teachers alike. Graeme, on the other hand, was a less experienced reader. Even though in this instance the older of the two children was the more mature reader, this was not always the case. Many of our Kindergarten and Grade One students were far more experienced with books than some of the children in Grade Two.

The boys began with a question which established their own agenda. Graeme wondered if one of the dinosaurs in an illustration was the same one that Shawn had described earlier during our class "Sharing Time". Shawn stated why he thought it was not and went on to explain why.

In listening to this taped conversation, the enthusiasm of the boys is apparent. Twice over the fifteen-minute talk, Shawn remarks, "This is amazing! I can't believe this! Some of these I never even heard of!" Both boys want to find out more about dinosaurs and other prehistoric animals. They turn the first few pages, each sharing observations and pieces of information which they believe to be true. The pictures are a common vehicle which allows both boys to discuss their ideas together. They talk about fossils and animals which are similar to those seen today (e.g., alligators, jelly fish, squid), and theories about how dinosaurs became extinct. Graeme states, "Oh-oh. This is one. The sun got too hot and it died."

Although Shawn gets caught up in his own excitement and cuts Graeme off several times, Graeme does attempt to model Shawn's ideas and comments.

The following is a brief excerpt from this conversation. Throughout the transcript, the actual text being read by the boys is indicated by words printed in upper case letters. Our comments are printed in parentheses to the right of the conversations.

S: Stegosaurus and Brontos—
   Brontosaurus. That's my
   favorite dinosaur!
G: Dinosaurs?

S: Ah well. Alph— Alphasaurus and Brontosaurus are my favorites. Tyrannosaurus! Look at the thing! Triceratops — Tsk. I can't believe this! Some of these I never even heard of!

(Shawn demonstrates more than just reading. He draws on his interests and relates back to his prior knowledge.)

G: I — I know one that I never even heard of. . . that one and where's it? . . . that one.

(Graeme models not only Shawn's actual speech pattern but also his awareness that reading involves reflection.)

S: I haven't either. I've seen him. Look at that! *That's a —*

G: *a polar bear!*

S: No it isn't. [reading] MODERN HORSE-THREE TOES-FOUR TOES-ONE TOE-*THREE TOES.*

(The boys are sharing knowledge from their past experiences.)

G: *TODAY*—TO it says TODAY MILLION YEARS AGO. Uh. . .

S: THE FIRST HORSE HAD FOUR TOES ON ITS FRONT FEET.

G: No it has *three.*

S: *AND THREE* TOES ON ITS BACK FEET. MILLIONS OF YEARS LATER HORSES HAD THREE TOES ON EACH FOOT AND MIDDLE TOE WAS THE BIGGEST. TODAY HORSES HAVE ONE TOE ON EACH FOOT. IT IS CALLED A HOOF. So the hoof is their toe.

(Shawn models his ability to skim over information quickly, saying only the main ideas aloud. He goes back to read each sentence and ignores Graeme's attempt to slowly read one fact. He continues to read all of the information on horses' toes for his own clarification as well as Graeme's. Shawn is providing Graeme with access to information he would not otherwise acquire from investigating the pictures and text by himself.) (Shawn is drawing conclusions and internalizing new information.)

S: [correcting] MAMMOTH. . . Oh! What's underneath this?

G: Oh! That's . . . that's called man.

S: Those are cavemen. Yeah. Those are cavemen.

G: Caveman! — Captain Caveman!

S: That's a mammoth. That's a mammoth — some kind of a mammoth. I saw it in my cyclopaedia.

G: And that's all the dinosaurs!

S: Look at that. That's man. Now look at these things. Pterodac— he's bigger 'n — Pterodactyl's bigger 'n even him. Wow!

G: I know. So is this!

S: Yeah.

(Graeme is drawing on prior knowledge of his own.)
(Shawn draws on prior knowledge and uses it to validate information for Graeme.)
(Graeme is tiring of the topic.)

(Shawn succeeds in drawing Graeme back into the investigation of the pictures and text and further extends both of their understanding and analysis.)

Conclusion

The main objective of making observations of children's talk and modeling strategies in a multi-age grouping was certainly met in transcriptions such as the one above. We noticed not only the many different kinds of talk used by the two boys but also how the novice reader actually does model the demonstrations of the more capable reader. The older child uses talk to clarify ideas for the younger student as well as for himself.

It is interesting to note the higher levels of thinking (analysis, synthesis, evaluation) which are also evident in the conversation. The boy's oral language reveals that they are aware of a world beyond their immediate surroundings — an important sign of cognitive development. While this was not an original objective of our inquiry, it raises questions for further investigation.

Children have a natural sense of wonder about things and we can learn a great deal about how they make sense of their world through careful observation and lots of listening. Together they "construct meaning through collaboration", as Gordon Wells puts it. This happens when talk is a natural part of their reading and not just the calling-out of words from the printed page. Children are naturally interested in books, and we have observed many changes in their attitudes and comfort levels over the course of each term as they read and talk as a "family". They view themselves as readers and writers and they build confidence through the medium they know best — talk.

Classroom Story Talk: The Challenges Facing the Teacher

JANE THOMSON

Over the past few years, I have learned to appreciate the important role that stories have to play in the educational, social, and emotional development of children. By interweaving their life experiences with their understanding of a text, students create a new interpretation of the story that has meaning for them. This process can be enhanced if the students are given an opportunity to share their interpretation of the story with other students. This interaction allows them to integrate other students' ideas and interpretations with their own, creating a deeper understanding of the story. The role of the teacher is to provide the context to facilitate this talk.

In the fall of 1989, I had the opportunity to do classroom research as part of my involvement in the TALK Project. I immediately decided to examine the effectiveness of "story talk" in my Grade One ESL classroom.

I videotaped and audiotaped the class talking about a variety of stories throughout the winter of 1990. As I reviewed the videotapes, I was shocked to find that the most apparent factor affecting the quality of story talk in my classroom was the way in which I, the teacher, interacted with the students. The videotapes from early in the research project indicated that my actions were hindering the development of meaningful talk. My approach towards the students changed as I viewed successive videotapes, and, as a result, later tapes show the talk becoming more meaningful and creative as the students strived to formulate and communicate ideas.

This paper will examine how a teacher's actions can either help or hinder the development of meaningful talk about stories. Two videotapes will be featured. The first was filmed early in the research project while I conducted a discussion about beaches prior to reading aloud *Do Not Open* by Brinton Turkel. (The story is about a woman who finds a bottle washed up on shore. The label — "Do not open" — does not dissuade her, and she releases an evil spirit who does great damage until she cleverly gets rid of him.) The videotape highlights teacher actions that hinder the development of meaningful talk. The second videotape was filmed later in the project after the story *Do Not Open* had been read several times and various follow-up activities had been completed. In it the students attempt to solve the problem of how Miss Moodie's banjo clock got fixed. This videotape demonstrates teacher actions which can facilitate the development of meaningful talk among students.

The First Videotape: A Pre-reading Discussion about Beaches

At the start of this lesson, the students, many of them of oriental origin, eagerly contributed their ideas about what might be found on a beach. They answered from their own experiences, using their knowledge of what is found on Asian beaches, including how turtles bury their eggs:

TEACHER: What would you find on the beach?
VU: A crab.
KWAN CHON: A shark.
VU: I find a turtle on the sand, um, a baby . . . in beach and small cover a egg and egg crack. . .
KWAN CHON: Its mom put it in there and she hide it, don't let somebody took it.

The context the students were able to work within (Asian beaches) was not the context that I was prepared to work within (North American beaches). As the discussion failed to proceed in the direction that I wanted it to, I spoke more and more, and my questions became longer and more directed. As a result, the students became confused and their contributions became shorter:

TEACHER: What I want you to try and think of is things, not animals, but just things you find lying on the beach.
VU: A turtle.
TEACHER: Okay, let's pretend grade ones, let's pretend there's a boat. There's a boat right out here, okay? The boat's out here [gestures with hands] and the boat capsizes, it turns upside down, and all the things fall out of the boat. What kinds of things could be pushed on to the beach from the boat?
KWAN CHON: It might be the turtle she push it.

In addition, my responses to the students' ideas were not consistent. I responded to what I considered "good" ideas with enthusiasm ("Oh! Kwan Chon! Where would a branch come from?") and to what I considered "off topic" answers with a "Maybe". The students, realizing that I was looking for a specific, "correct" answer, lost confidence in their ideas, and contributed short, one-word answers to the discussion:

VU: Turtle.
TEACHER: Maybe.
IVA: Um . . . frog.
TEACHER: Maybe.

In the end, I had spoken four times as much as the students, and very little meaningful talk had taken place.

The Second Videotape: A Post-reading Discussion about a Clock

This lesson turned out to be very different from the one I had planned. I had intended to have the students look for unsolved problems in *Do Not Open*. As an example, I mentioned the problem that I had identified: "How did the banjo clock get fixed?" At this point, instead of looking for more problems in the story, the students started using their imaginations to extend the story and create an answer to my problem. In this videotape, my agenda was flexible. I followed the interests of the students and we had a long, absorbing discussion about the repair of the banjo clock.

Instead of being long and directed, my questions in the second videotape were short and open-ended. The students were given time to think, respond to, and build upon each other's ideas. The discussion was meaningful to them and they understood where it was going. Their contributions became longer, and reflected comprehension of the discussion as a whole:

TEACHER: How did the clock get fixed?
TRUNG: I know . . . the monster did it.
TUAN: Maybe, maybe the monster.
TRUNG: But the monster just stay in the bottle day. . . when somebody eat him. . .
TUAN: But now it do work.
IVA: The monster fix it.

My role in this discussion was not that of a leader but of a facilitator, helping the students to create a story that was their own. I supplied needed vocabulary to smoothe the flow of conversation:

TUAN: He takes something and put it in there and close it, and what's her name again?
TEACHER: Miss Moodie.
TUAN: Miss Moodie hear the bong bong.

I provided openings for the students to contribute their ideas in order to ensure that the discussion reflected the ideas of the group as a whole ("What do you have to say, Iva?"). And I asked for clarification when I thought the meaning of a particular contribution was unclear. This forced the students to make sure what they said made sense:

TRUNG: Yeah, the baby the baby the monster.
TEACHER: Wait a second, he [the monster] had a baby?
TUAN: No, he was a baby just in the bottle and he saw the smoke and he grow bigger.

The talk was cooperative. The students strived to communicate, despite their limited language ability, because it was important for them to convey their ideas. For them, the communication of ideas became far more important than the way the ideas were expressed; they were willing to take risks in order to be understood. When this happens, the ability to manipulate language improves rapidly.

Conclusion

In the first videotape I had my own agenda which I wanted to complete. I was looking for specific answers based on what might be found on a North American beach. The talk that resulted was not real to the students because it did not relate to their own experiences and ideas.

In order for the talk to be real and cooperative, the teacher must be a facilitator, making it clear to the students that they are teaching and learning together. In this role, the teacher must have a flexible agenda, following the students' interests and ideas.

In the second videotape, I guided the discussion from behind, by providing openings, helping with vocabulary, and asking for clarification. I was careful to ask short, open-ended questions and give the students time to think and respond to each other. This is, I think, one of the most important challenges that continues to face me as a teacher: to listen to the students, taking cues from them and using their needs and interests as a focal point for future plans.

Talk and Peer Conferencing in the Writing Process
ANNE KRANT

My inquiry began as a result of my dissatisfaction with certain aspects of my Grade Three writing program — in particular, the lack of meaningful talk during peer group conferencing. Videotaping done at the beginning of the school year indicated that there was very little constructive talk going on during these meetings. The talk consisted primarily of "That's good", "I liked your story", "This needs a capital", "Put a period here", etc. It was obvious that the children were not really talking about their work and that strategies were needed to help them make the transitions from author to reader to listener to critic.

After reading several articles related to various writing programs, I found the book entitled *Creating Classrooms for Authors* by Jerome Harste, Kathy C. Short, and Carolyn Burke most helpful. Their process, called the "Authoring Cycle", which includes "Author's Folder", "Author's Circle", "Author's Chair", and "Editor's Table" as ingredients in a writing program, seemed to come closest to what I was already doing in the classroom and suggested ways in which it might be improved. The idea of the Author's Circle in particular seemed a viable means by which to elicit the kind of talk I was after. Everyone who attends the circle must bring a rough draft of writing and is there because they want to think and talk about their particular piece with others. The circle usually consists of three or four students.

I decided to examine interactions in authors' circles to see what worked and what didn't. In the end, I focused on four factors that seem to promote talk during peer conferencing: establishing the purpose of the conference; assuming ownership; questioning; and making the reading/writing connection.

Establishing the Purpose of the Conference

When children were asked to help another child or group of children with their writing, they automatically assumed they were supposed to correct errors in spelling, grammar, and vocabulary. This was very evident during the taping sessions.

MARTIN: Oh God, look how much mistakes you made. This is wrong, this is wrong.

Only occasionally did the real purpose of the meeting come to the surface:

MARTIN: Let's see if we can make it make sense. You have a problem here.

The true purpose of any conference must be made clear. The purpose of the Author's Circle lends itself to talk; students are there for reactions and feedback to their writing with the focus on meaning, not "correctness". Editing must be seen as a totally separate and different part of the process.

I suggest that talk can play a major role in a child's transition from thinking about a story to actually writing it. Watch children during writing time and often they can be seen talking even to themselves about what they are producing. This substantiates my feeling that talk is really thinking out loud and a prerequisite to the writing process.

The Author's Circle can then be seen not only as a place to share finished products but also as a forum at which authors can discuss any problems they may be having. Peer conferencing can be extremely useful when children are "stuck" as to where to go in their stories. Giving children an opportunity to discuss their writing could be labeled by some traditionalists as non-productive since they view the lack of substantial written work as evidence of a lack of learning. But what may seem to be "just talk" can lead children to suggest, develop, and try various writing strategies. Listening and questioning draw words out, and writers quite often find themselves saying things they didn't know they knew. Teachers can help by respecting the thinking process as much as the final outcome.

One of the criteria of the Author's Circle is that everyone must bring a rough draft of writing. It need not be a complete piece. I highly recommend that the teacher also share his or her writing with the group as well. The teacher's role as a participant sets the tone for the type of exchange that will occur. Many specialists believe that children learn by imitation and that teachers need to provide models. Instead of merely teaching certain skills, teachers can model and demonstrate them.

Even the physical arrangement or organization of the conference setting can enhance talk and discussion. I have found that using a round table, for example, works very well. Conference groups should be flexible and not always involve large groups. Sharing with a partner often allows students who are shy or somewhat unsure of their writing ability to gain confidence and practice in conferencing so that they are better able to contribute effectively during larger group situations.

The Author's Circle format also helps children make the shift from author to critic in a workable, meaningful way, without getting defensive, but rather listening to feedback, taking notes, and later deciding for themselves what to do with information they receive. The idea of the teacher sharing his or her own writing too makes it clear that the teacher is merely a participant, not *the* critic. As a result, students may feel freer to make their own revision choices rather than simply doing what the teacher suggests. Teachers must show students how to revise so that improving a story is not looked upon as an overwhelming rewriting of the entire story. Some practical suggestions include: 1) having the students write on every other line so that there is room for additions and changes; 2) using only one side of the paper so that larger additions can be made on the other side; 3) teaching students the proper use of arrows and asterisks for additions; and 4) actually cutting strips of paper and glueing them onto the revised sections. (My students, however, found this last suggestion too much work.)

If, after having shared their stories at the Author's Circle and made their revisions, they wish to publish their pieces, they should then take them to the Editor's Table. The editors consist of children who volunteer for the job each week. Their task is to concentrate only on the conventions — spelling, punctuation, and grammar. No changes may be made without consultation with the author. This way, the concern for conventions is kept entirely separate from the conferencing for content only. Even this process of editing encourages talk, because if something is unclear the editors must go back to the author and discuss the problem.

51

Assuming Ownership

One of the most important things a child must do is to assume and maintain ownership of his or her own piece throughout the writing process. This involves reading it to an audience. With short pieces it is often helpful to read it once so that the listeners can get the main gist of the story, and then again so that the listeners may focus more on how the meaning is achieved. Having the author read the piece also eliminates situations in which readers must struggle with such things as untidy printing, invented spelling, and grammatical errors. As previously mentioned, the purpose of the conference is to focus on content and this is difficult to do if you are bogged down in the reading of a text. The following excerpt from videotaping clearly demonstrates this point. Martin begins reading Jun's story.

> MARTIN: "The dinosaur bones is at the museum." I'm not sure you spelled that right. Uh, what's this? Is this an r? There's no such word.

Martin continues reading.

> Is this all one word? "It came alive and lade an egg." That's not how you spell laid.
> JUN: Here, let me read it.
> MARTIN: No, I'll just cross it out.

Martin obviously could not respond to the text. As he was reading, he was becoming acutely aware of all the mistakes and naturally focused on conventions. We sense Martin's impatience with the text, but even more so Jun's frustration at hearing Martin stumbling through his story. Realizing the difficulty for themselves, the boys began to read the story together, and this produced more successful results and led to more meaningful talk. When the author maintains ownership, all partners are actively involved as either listeners or readers. Videotaping sessions done in early September in which one student read another's story clearly show that once a sense of ownership is lost, the children tend to just sit there, bored, waiting for the other pupil(s) to finish reading.

Another instance that shows the advantages of having the author read in order to make the meaning clear is as follows.

Martin has been reading Jun's story.

MARTIN: Wait, there's one thing mysterious about this. You said
the dinosaur bones is at the museum, right? "And I built the
bones together." And who did you build it with?
JUN: Nobody.
MARTIN: Then how come you said together?
JUN: Like, here's the bones, you put it together. [demonstrates
with his hands]

Had Jun initially read his own story this confusion over the
word "together" might not have occurred in the first place. The
author knows what the intent is and where to put the emphasis.

The second advantage of having authors read their own stories
is that it helps improve the listening skills of the audience. Each
member of the Author's Circle is asked to respond to the piece,
so critical listening is important. Later in the above taping session, Jun's fight for ownership resulted in some good talk and
subsequent learning. Martin didn't know how to spell the name
of one of the dinosaurs, so he tried to convince Jun to just change
the name of it. He then proceeded to spell another dinosaur's
name. Jun refused to give in and together the boys went off in
search of dinosaur books and eventually found the correct spelling. It has been said that writing involves risk-taking, and Martin would rather have played it safe by using something he was
sure of. I had to admire Jun's tenacity, and the tape revealed
a side of him not normally seen.

After the writer has read his or her story, each of the participants is given an opportunity to respond to it. They don't
even see the text, so they are not bogged down by invented spelling and other mistakes. It is sometimes suggested that copies
of the draft be given to the members of the Circle, particularly
with longer stories. I avoided doing this in the early stages and
would not be inclined to attempt it with primary children. If
nothing else, keeping the draft in the hands of the author rein-
forces ownership.

Questioning

The next important strategy for promoting talk during the conference groups is appropriate questioning. Above all, we must
make sure that the questions are not directed at fault-finding.
Primary children coming to the Circle usually like their pieces

and often feel they represent their best efforts, so other members of the Circle should be asked not to offer harsh judgmental comments but rather to try to be helpful and improve upon the quality of the writing. The other members of the Circle are there for supportive criticism — a difficult concept to foster. The teacher can help by making some initial comments and setting the tone for others to follow. The teacher must also be alert and observe the effects of the group's questions and/or comments on each writer. When questions are not helpful, the teacher may need to intervene or ask questions of her own.

Questions should be directed so that they do not focus totally on areas of the writing that need improving. Too much advice or bare criticism can be overwhelming for the author. This was very obvious during one of the taping sessions between Martin and Jun when Martin was continually finding fault with Jun's story. In Martin's eagerness to help Jun, he became too critical and, at one point, too technical.

MARTIN: It came alive. I know, but how come you said it's bones, not skin? How could something be alive with just bones? It has to have flesh and blood inside. You get my point?

Jun's intention in his story was clearly concerned not with how things really are, but rather with being creative. At least Martin was sensitive enough to realize that Jun was just about to give up, because he said:

Don't erase it all because it's pretty good. I make mistakes. Long ago my teacher gave me a lot of corrections too.

He also sensed Jun's need for encouragement at another point in the conferencing session when Jun was making some necessary revisions. Martin made comments such as, "How's it going, Jun?" "Is it going okay?" "Where are you now?"

I found that making a statement to which children can relate is often a much better way of eliciting talk rather than asking specific questions. Having listeners tell what they heard in the story first creates a more positive atmosphere and is generally something all of them can do. If the children can respond to different parts of the story, the author feels he or she has successfully got a message across. If, however, the audience immediately begins asking questions, the author tends to become defensive and unsure of his or her ability as a writer.

54

During our peer conferencing, I have found the phrase "tell me" a very effective introduction to the discussion.

"Tell me one thing you remember from the story."
"Tell me about a particular part that caught your attention."
"Tell me about a character that you liked or didn't like."
"Tell me about your favorite part or a part that surprised you."

These statements all create a positive attitude towards the story and tend to lead to more productive talk as opposed to specific questions such as, "What part did you like best?" This type of questioning encourages a critical judgment, and in the early stages of conferencing the children are not ready for this. It is much simpler to be a listener first, then a critic.

After the listeners have commented on what they've heard or liked, then some questions can be raised as to how well the author said what he or she was actually trying to say.

What really enhances the talk is having the author answer questions about the story, forcing him or her to think about it. Often young children have complex thoughts in their heads but only put down a sketchy outline. As the children ask questions about parts that were confusing or unclear, it becomes more obvious to the author that more detail needs to be given in order for the meaning to be clear and the story to make sense to an audience. Demonstrating this is far more effective than "telling" it. I was reassured to read during my research that it takes time for children to understand how to receive and give constructive criticism. They are inexperienced critics, so teachers must provide demonstrations during the first few circles.

Susan Schwartz in her book *All Write* suggests some ways to help students formulate good questions. Early in the school year, the teacher brings in an object and tells the class that there is a story behind it. Instead of telling the story to the children, they draw the story out by asking questions such as "Who?" "What?" "Where?" "When?" These questions generally produce factual information, whereas "Why?" and "How?" produce much more interesting ideas.

The pupils are then given opportunities to practise this procedure in small groups, bringing in their own objects for discussion. Once students have become accustomed to this routine, they are encouraged to share their ideas during story writing time and to listen to one another's stories. Because of the questioning techniques which they have previously learned, this kind of discussion should improve all aspects of their writing. I like this idea not so much because it suggests which types of questions should be asked at the Author's Circle but because it suggests that when children learn to ask questions of each other, they may learn to ask questions and look for answers in their own texts.

Making the Reading/Writing Connection

In order to become good critics, children need many opportunities to be just that, and this can be achieved through daily read-aloud sessions. Much research has been done on the reading/writing connection. Several studies have shown that many of the skills used in the writing process are also used in reading, and that the skills and awareness of one process can be transferred to the other. Therefore, it is extremely advantageous to have reading and writing connected in the children's minds. We now begin our writing block each day with a story. It is helpful to choose one that features a particular aspect of literature such as humor, suspense, descriptive language, poetry, or good action. Through follow-up discussions we look at the various ways in which the author achieves his or her particular effect. This often results in insights the children can take back to their own writings. Exposing them to a wide variety of literature helps develop their skills as critics as well.

A pupil may also read his or her own published book — in the "Author's Chair" — and follow the reading with a question-and-comment period, which again can provide a framework and additional modeling for conference groups during the actual writing time. I try not to make a distinction between the reading of the children's writing and that of professionals.

Literature can also serve as a stimulus for students' writing, as they may borrow styles and even specific characters or partial plots from a book they have enjoyed reading or hearing. Many teachers in the primary grades use well known pattern books in exactly this way. Some children are naturally more creative than others, and reading can offer ideas to children who otherwise might have difficulty getting started.

Finally, the teacher's attitude towards reading and writing

can also have a profound affect on pupils. One who exudes a love of reading and rejoices in the published works of the class helps instil enthusiasm in the children.

Conclusion

I have spent considerable time this school year reading, researching, examining, and experimenting with a wide variety of ideas relating to the writing process. The strategies that I have presented in this paper appear to be commonly agreed upon by all the leading researchers and authors. They have convinced me of the importance of talk prior to, during, and after the actual writing experience. And talk shouldn't just mean that children talk more; teachers must listen more. The key to helping children become better writers is to let them know they have something important to say and that we are interested in hearing it. Listening is hard, and as teachers we often worry too much about running out of time or about asking the right questions — and so we forget to listen. Children will talk more if they find that the information they share is used to help them say more.

Peer conferencing skills don't just materialize overnight. The changes that have taken place in my classroom this year have been the culmination of several months of trial and error. When I actually put the whole procedure into practice, I found it worked relatively well. One important discovery I made was that it is vital to allow participants in the Author's Circle sufficient time to immediately go back and work on their revisions if they so wish. Otherwise, despite making little notes or using arrows, the feedback and suggestions made are no longer fresh in the children's minds and all the time spent talking does not result in any significant improvements to their writing.

I found that because thinking and sharing take time, it is best to keep the Author's Circle small and fluid. I have also used it as a brainstorming tool when a pupil is having trouble with a particular section or aspect of a story. It is often much easier for the teacher to simply make suggestions, but the benefit of having their peers talk out the problem and work out their own solutions is a very valuable learning experience for the children.

My advice to colleagues would be to let the children talk first and then help them by listening, modeling, and gently guiding.

As long as children talk, not only do we as teachers learn more about the subject, we gain a perspective on what will help each child.

Although my present class may not have reaped the benefits of my own increased knowledge and awareness, I feel confident that future classes will. I am eager to implement the strategies I have discussed here from the very beginning of the next school year in order to make peer conferencing a valuble tool in my writing program. I know one thing for sure: my classroom won't be as quiet as it used to be.

3. Talk across the Curriculum: Talk as a Way of Learning in Every Subject

Traditionally, speaking and listening activities have been part of the language arts portion of the curriculum. However, as a medium of communication and exchange, talk occurs in all areas of the curriculum: children working on a science experiment dialogue constantly as they try to understand each new component that affects the work; amateur archaeologists engage in conversation as they unearth hidden dinosaur bones in the sandbox; girls and boys discuss contemporary problems in guidance sessions. And yet, while using talk as a natural mode of learning in all the various disciplines, teachers have seldom examined its nature and assessed the ways in which children could be assisted in increasing their potential for talk within the context of different subjects. Many teachers in the TALK Project began to look at how talk worked in subjects other than language arts.

In her Junior Kindergarten classroom, Eunice Cott observed the language of one of her five-year-old students at various activity centres and talk situations. She tape-recorded, transcribed, and assessed the child's talk in order to reflect on the languaging processes she noticed. Eunice found this to be an informative way to build a picture of a child, noting his or her growth as a guide for her actions and reactions as a teacher. She learned that language appraisal does not mean categorizing a child, but rather building a cumulative picture.

Theme-related talk in Kindergarten was the focus of an inquiry by Lyn Mann and Tracy Murray. Their work was based on Brian Cambourne's structural framework outlined in *The Whole Story*. They were both aware of the value of play, but their work helped them realize that the level and quality of talk can be enriched by focusing on the context of the learning situation. They found that too many children's needs were overlooked for the personal curriculum needs of the teachers. Adults must take care that they intervene carefully at the activity

59

centres and support child conversation with relevant and appropriate responses, giving both assurance and feedback to the tentative language risks children are taking. Lyn and Tracy focused their observations on the needs of the children and in doing so, demonstrated how learners make sense of their new ideas and understanding.

Pam Goring had just returned to the profession, and needed to be convinced that the computer programs being presented to children were worthwhile as a way of learning. She was concerned that the children were not communicating with each other while working together. Using the program "Dragon's Keep", Pam videotaped conversations at the computer, transcribed them, and analysed the data. She was surprised at the degree of success the children had in performing tasks, and saw that they do get on with a task as long as the program motivates them. The peer teaching that took place provided her with justification for using computer programs in a learning environment, and made her more aware of the personalities of the children she was grouping together. By listening more attentively to the conversation at the computer, Pam feels she will be more able to assess the learning that is taking place.

Talking and Cooperating

DEBBIE GIBSON, LORI MATTAROLLO, JIM VINCENT

The purpose of the "Talking and Cooperating Project" was to enhance the mathematics program by providing an environment where peers could help each other learn more about fractions.

As a result of our observations we perceived that students who characteristically performed at a lower achievement level in mathematics improved their understanding of fractional concepts after talking with students who usually performed at a relatively high level. We sensed that students who were allowed to talk seemed less frustrated while solving problems than students we had taught in the past who were not encouraged to talk.

We wanted students to have a lasting understanding of the concepts of fractions. This led to the following questions, which initially directed our study:

1. What approach do we take?
2. How do we enhance communication skills?
3. How do we maximize group participation?
4. How do we acquire materials to do this?
5. What materials do we use to evaluate the process?

Background

The idea for this project originated through discussions of ways to enrich the mathematics program. We examined many materials, such as pattern blocks, designed to improve the understanding of fractions. We looked for activities that promoted active learning in an environment where, according to Deineka, Hunt, and Pogue (1986), "children are encouraged to investigate, think, judge, appreciate, imagine, feel, enjoy, and create".

At workshops we had experimented with problem-solving activities with an emphasis on communication through group sharing. These initial experiences led us to develop a unit of study that would focus on talk, hands-on activities, and problem-solving tasks that would emphasize peer sharing. We discussed various ways all students could experience success in mathematics.

Methodology

We ranked one Grade Four and one Grade Five class's mathematic achievement levels so we could set up heterogeneous groups. Each group was made up of three or four students who started by creating group names. We set up our heterogeneous groups with one student who characteristically performed mathematics at a lower achievement level, one student who performed at a higher level, and two students who usually displayed average mathematical achievements.

After consultation with a mathematics resource person, we selected learning materials for the two grade levels that contained problem-solving activities. We chose to use pattern blocks as our concrete manipulatives. It was expected that students would discover the concepts through manipulation and reinforce them through discussion. The students were introduced to the materials through free play. We encouraged them to begin cooperative work and oral communication by presenting them with tasks that required dialogue — for example, "As partners, create a design. . ."

The Team Game Tournament

We chose to call this activity the "Team Game Tournament". We wanted the students to have a discovery opportunity before receiving the teacher's instructions, and we wanted to keep teacher instruction to a minimum.

We provided a game situation to see if students would transfer their understanding of mathematical concepts to new situations. We changed the groups and made them more homogeneous in nature. Students then competed individually with members of other groups, and were awarded points on an individual basis. The students then returned to their original groups to find out their group scores.

Groups were rewarded for their efforts with certificates posted in their classrooms. We acknowledged the groups who worked well together and the groups who accumulated the highest scores.

Students participating in the project were videotaped at the beginning, middle, and end of it. We recorded an audiotape of the conversations that took place between the students to better analyse the talk interactions.

Observations

Six themes emerged from the student conversations: sharing, guessing, agreeing, risk-taking, teaching, and spelling.

1. Sharing
The following exchange shows a group sharing a dicovery and an activity.

ALICE AND BARB: Yeah, yeah, you're right!
ALICE: I knew it was blue when it had to be one!
BARB: Okay.
   [Alice and Barb laugh.]
COLIN: What are you doing here?
ALICE: I did it.
BARB: Okay.
COLIN: I have 1, 2, 3, 4, 5, yup. Let's put these back in.
BARB: Okay.

COLIN: You're coloring yellow.

2. Guessing
In this exchange, the children are making guesses about a particular problem.

BARB: How about, um. . . I think I know. I think . . . it's green.
COLIN: I think I know.
ALICE: It has to be number five.
BARB: Yeah, I think it's green.
COLIN: Then probably green.
ALICE: No, it can't be. No, it can't be.
BARB: Then probably these.
COLIN: Wait, we'll try this.
BARB: No, no, it isn't. It isn't done.
ALICE: The ends were taken up.
ALICE: I knew it had to be blue when it was one.

3. Agreeing
Sometimes the talk simply confirms agreement.

KRIS: It equals one. Right?
ADAM: Right.
HIRO: Okay.
KARI: Let's move on.

4. Risk-taking
In this excerpt, Kris takes a risk.

ADAM: One yellow equals four red.
KARI: I don't know.
KRIS: No, I think that one yellow equals two red.
ADAM: Oh. . . well. . . um. . . I guess you're right.
ADAM: Okay.

5. Teaching
In this exchange, Kris teaches Hiro. It is worth noting that Hiro usually performs much better in mathematics tests than do Kris and Kari.

ADAM: One half is red.
KRIS: No, we use blue.
KARI: Two wholes, no — two halves, I mean two halves equal six green.
HIRO: No you're wrong.
KRIS: Yes it does. Watch this, Hiro. See if you can do this, Hiro.
[Hiro plays with the blocks and sees that the girls were right.]

6. Spelling

The following is a typical exercise in spelling in order to solve the task at hand.

COLIN: The denominator. What does it mean?
ALICE: One whole, it means. It means one whole.
BARB: No, the total pieces. Like all they have together.
COLIN: I'm looking up there at the blackboard.
ALICE: Just put total. T-O-T-A-L and number of pieces.
COLIN: P-I-C- no P-I-C?
BARB: Oh, yeah.
ALICE: P-I-E
   [All laugh.]
BARB: P-I-E-C.
COLIN: C-E-S.
ALICE AND COLIN: I-E-C-E-S.
BARB: Little pieces. I finally got it. Right?
COLIN: Or the denominator.

During our observations, we noticed several problems — and some improvements and possible solutions.

First, it was a challenge to get students to share materials and space. (Perhaps this will always be true!)

At first, it was a challenge to get students to agree when one student dominated the group. As the groups progressed, however, more cooperation was evident and no one individual took charge.

Students were reluctant to put answers on paper. It seemed they did not want to gamble on answers that might not be correct. We sensed that more students were willing to take chances when they were given the option of answering verbally without being confined to print. We perceived that a freer exchange of ideas came about through oral interaction. We sense this brought about a willingness to take risks.

Curiously, it was difficult for students who characteristically performed well on mathematics tests to express themselves, while students who usually performed poorly on mathematics tests sometimes ended up teaching their "brighter" peers how to solve problems. They seemed to have a much better grasp of the concrete materials.

The discipline focus was mathematics, but that did not stop a natural transfer to language and the spelling out of words used in the problem-solving sessions.

Conclusions

As teacher questioning techniques improved, we sensed that our students' questions improved. We believe there was a role model transfer as the mode of communication changed from one of giving answers to one of bringing about the discovery of relationships. At first our questions were very shallow, directed at specific answers. As we improved our questioning skills, we also improved our abilities to explain and discuss relationships with each other.

We look at the curriculum differently after this project. We found from first-hand experience that students should discover concepts for themselves rather than be taught them directly. By setting up problems where students could discover relationships, we believe we enhanced the participants' oral risk-taking behaviors. As students willingly shared their ideas, not afraid to make mistakes, they became better risk-takers and problem-solvers. The Ontario Ministry of Education Language Across the Curriculum Guidelines (1978) state that: "in every subject area students require frequent opportunities for exploratory talk and small group discussion to put new information and ideas into their own words". We agree.

As we observed the students in their groups and reviewed their work or end products, we saw ourselves being more patient, thus allowing students more time to deal with the work themselves rather than interjecting too quickly. We sense it is always a challenge for teachers to ascertain the amount of time students need to struggle with a concept before the teachers get involved and guide the students through the concepts themselves. We felt this was a significant learning experience which made us rethink our teaching behaviors and patterns.

We became better observers and as a result felt more confident about evaluating the students' level of understanding. We watched and listened to them in action. This opportunity enriched our vision of the students' potential abilities in other learning situations. How could students who consistently perform poorly on achievement tests be better utilized in group settings as catalysts for their own and other group members' learning (as Kris and Kari taught Hiro)?

There were several significant findings projected from this talking and cooperating study. We perceived that students needed to use hands-on materials with time to explore and discuss their ideas more completely. In the past we gave students pencil and paper tests; we did not allow a free exchange of ideas; it was apparent that students did not understand some concepts; we did not expect them to vocalize their understandings.

Our goal was to ensure that students understood the concepts by dealing with concrete objects. Virtually all students seemed to grasp ideas that they could work with physically.

Benefits of Cooperative Approach

Students appeared to enjoy what they were doing as they experienced success. All participants became better observers and questioners. We began to realize what questions evoked appropriate thought and response to the problems at hand. This enabled us to become better learners and facilitators as the students progressed through their tasks.

We believe talk is a vital component of any mathematical program. By listening to the children communicate we could trace oral and aural understanding which seemed to foster overall understanding of concepts. We feel that one truly does not comprehend something until he or she can verbally express it. As Pericles once said, "He who cannot express what he thinks is at the level of he who cannot think."

Each group discussion was quite unique. There did not appear to be any set pattern for problem-solving. Furthermore, cooperative learning in heterogeneous groups appeared to be beneficial for all participants in this project.

Future Focus

There are several areas we would like to continue exploring:

How can we utilize this approach effectively in other areas of mathematics?

Can we apply cooperative learning strategies effectively to other subjects in the school curriculum?

Is there a relationship between self-esteem and cooperative learning?

Is there a relationship between motivation and cooperative learning?

How are cooperative learning strategies incorporated into teacher preparation and professional development programs?

In conclusion, this cooperative learning experience increased our understanding of how students learn in dynamic group situations. We were pleased to see that the students appeared to enjoy participating in the project. We believe that through this interactive experience students understood more about the mathematical concepts of fractions. "Talking and Cooperating" was truly a growth experience for all.

Talk and Computers

JOHN FORTH AND CATHERINE MORRISON

In this initial inquiry it was our intent to explore the relationship between talk and the use of computers. The central question we posed was: Are computers an effective medium for the development of oral language in the young child?

Our method of investigation was to involve a variety of student groups in computer activity and then observe the quantity and quality of their talk. The groups were recorded on videotape. Student samples included the following groupings:

1. Grade One: four students, male and female.
2. Grade Three: three students, male and female.
3. Grade Five/Six: six students, male and female.

The computer programs utilized in this inquiry included a cross-section of subject areas which can be divided into several groupings:

1. drill and practice.
2. interactive reading/writing.
3. problem-solving.
4. simulation.

Observations

We found that children engaged in much conversation around the computer. Several types of talk were observed — social, interactive, collaborative, predicting, and problem-solving. All participants were very enthusiastic about computer activity.

67

Conclusion

In the course of this inquiry we made a number of interesting discoveries. We hope to further explore several of these findings in subsequent investigations related to the TALK Project. Among other things, we found the following:

1. Computers serve as an excellent tool for the development of social, intellectual, emotional, and creative growth.
2. Computer talk facilitates and enhances social group interaction, joint problem-solving, and decision-making, as well imaginative thought and creative language.
3. Group computer activity fosters the building of self-esteem through collaborative effort and immediate feedback from the computer.
4. Few educational experiences are more effective in stimulating and sustaining student interest and motivation than working with a computer. We found that students who did not respond well to traditional academic activity were often particularly interested in computer activity.
5. The quality and quantity of talk around a computer is significantly influenced by the selection of software. For example, we found that simulation programs requiring interpretation and speculation generated an abundance of communicative exchange; conversely, drill programs tended to generate minimal talk.

These conclusions have inspired us to further pursue and extend the focus of this inquiry. It is evident on the basis of our initial inquiry that computers can act as a catalyst for young children in developing oral language.

Positive Talk to Promote Self-Esteem and Learning

NANCY TURNER

My ultimate goal as a teacher of children with learning disabilities is to rebuild their fragile self-image. By the age of ten they have experienced failure for most of their school lives, and their self-esteem is low. This low self-image is expressed in many ways, from acting out to get attention, to withdrawing into silence to avoid it.

When I agreed to participate in the TALK Project, I felt that the limited abilities and problems of my students set limits on my venues of study. I also wanted the project to enhance my program and be an integral part of it, and that set limits too.

Since oral language was the most used form of instruction in my class, I decided to read a novel out loud to the whole class, even though they were all at different reading levels. My first attempt to read a novel to this group was recorded and the results provided me with my project thesis: "The reinforcement of positive talk and the use of positive talk will result in the improvement of self-esteem and therefore result in improved learning ability."

Pupils Involved

There were eight students — six boys and two girls — ages nine to eleven. All were communication-disabled, ranging from level one to almost level five in reading, spelling, and language skills.

One boy, Dale, had come to the class after spending three and a half years in behavior modification classes in Etobicoke and Peel schools. This child was verbally abusive and destructive to his peers. He typically said things like, "You're ugly," "You're stupid," "I don't like you," and "Who'd want you for a friend?"

Once, in front of both girls in the class, Dale said to one of them, "Why do you care? She [the other girl] told me on the bus that she doesn't like you anyway. She did! She told me!" When the girl he was speaking to burst into tears, he said, "I didn't know she'd cry." He couldn't comfort her or say he was sorry. He had no social skills to help him be less hurtful.

Not only did Dale berate his peers, he also talked baby talk, constantly interrupted, wandered around the room, and took others' belongings and destroyed them. His file indicated level one skills across all areas except mathematics computations.

On the plus side, Dale was nice looking, healthy, physically active, and of average size. He was well traveled and had extensive knowledge of antiques from trips with his mother, who had an avid interest in antiques.

I used this project to provide Dale and his classmates with the necessary tools to interact appropriately with peers and other information sharers to try to elimate negative talk.

We began reading Roald Dahl's novel, *The Witches*, in early

October. Over the next couple of weeks, I read aloud from the book regularly. What follows are some episodes and exchanges that took place during the reading, and my thoughts on them.

October 13, 1988

> LOCATION: on the carpet at the front of the classroom, children in relaxed positions. Tape recorder on floor nearby.

I read the introduction, asking questions as I read.

> TEACHER: What is this book going to be about?
> [Results very disappointing. The children clapped, hummed, interrupted, and giggled. Their answers had no bearing on the story.]

October 14, 1988

I played the tape from the previous day back to the children and asked them how they felt about it.

> PUPIL 1: I felt it was really bad. . . all that noise Andrew and Dale made.
> PUPIL 2: Bad I guess, because people were silly and stuff.
> PUPIL 3: It was okay, but without the noises it would have been better.
> PUPIL 4: I don't know, it would have been better if everyone hadn't been fooling around. I sounded funny on the tape. I hate talking on tape.
> PUPIL 5: I feel bad about it because people kept making rude noises and stuff and you couldn't hear anything. It would have been good if everyone would have been quiet.
> PUPIL 6: I felt I was making too much noise and I shouldn't have and other people were making weird noises and shouldn't have.
> DALE: It was fun doing it, but it turned out dumb because people were silly, I was silly. If we do another tape, it'll be better because I won't be silly.
> PUPIL 8: Comme ci, comme ça.

October 15, 1988

This time I changed the location. Near the back of the room, we sat around a large table with the tape recorder in the centre of the table. I felt a more structured location might help pupils to attain more self-control during the session.

I began to read, and Dale interrupted: "Brrrr dadada . . . I know what's happening . . . I know what's going to happen, eeeah."

TEACHER: Dale, would you please wait until I read and then let the rest of us think about it and come up with our own answers?

DALE: I don't know how much dirt you get from a gerbil!

[Teacher continues to read, making no comment.]

DALE: [While teacher is reading] Oooh, brrr, tatata, oooh, brrrrr, teehee, teehee. . .

[Teacher ignores him and varies tone, reading more softly. Dale continues making noises and interruptions. Teacher continues reading. The chapter is about how you can spot a real witch. One indicator is that she has blue saliva, described as phlegm.]

TEACHER: What is phlegm?

DALE: [Speaks out without raising hand] Spit!

TEACHER: Would you please raise your hand next time Dale?

DALE: Yes.

[Teacher continues reading. Dale laughs and giggles and makes nonsense sounds. Teacher continues to read, varying voice tone but ignoring Dale's interruptions. Dale continues mimicking teacher, but not as often.

TEACHER: [At the end of a very exhausting reading session] Sometimes I wish I was a witch.

DALE: Aurgh!

[The end of that day's session.]

Dale seemed to be tiring, and his classmates, annoyed at his interruptions, had begun to ask him to stop. The structured setting at the table didn't seem to make a significant difference to Dale's behavior.

October 16, 1988

We returned to the original location, and students assumed a relaxed position on the carpet. The only stipulation was eye contact: they must watch the teacher.

One new element had been introduced: A moveable screen was placed at the back of the room with a student desk behind it, henceforth called "the office". Anyone who had difficulty cooperating could sit in this "office" and listen to the story from there. He/she would not be allowed to participate as part of the group. The first person to act silly, interrupt, or make weird or rude sounds would listen to the story from "the office".

[Teacher reads for a while.]

TEACHER: Please describe grandmother.

71

DALE: [Speaks out] She was wrinkled.

TEACHER: Hand, Dale!

DALE: [Raises hand]

TEACHER: Yes, Dale.

DALE: She was wrinkled.

TEACHER: Great! What was she wearing?

DALE: Ooh, ooh, ohh . . . lacka, lacka. . . oooh, oooh [waving hand in teacher's face, babbling while others try to answer] Lice, lice, lice.

[Teacher talks to another child.]

DALE: Are these lice?

[Rest of the class cries, "It's lace, Dale, she has on a lace dress."]

DALE: Lice? Lice?

TEACHER: [Ignoring Dale's play with words] What does lace look like?

[One of the girls has some on a blouse and shows it.]

TEACHER: May we continue?

DALE: Eeyeah.

[Dale is allowed to occupy the office for the rest of the session. Teacher completes the chapter with no interruptions.]

It was taking so long to get through a chapter or segment of reading because Dale was constantly interrupting that for several days Dale spent most of his listening time "not sharing" and in "the office", until he respected the rights of the others to have some of the teacher's attention. His exclusion seemd to make a difference to the story retention of his classmates — for the better. They remembered more of Dahl's imagery when questioned, and talked more about what they were hearing.

October 21, 1988

TEACHER: Let's review the part we read yesterday. Something very sad happened at the beginning of the chapter. What was it?

DALE: [Hand up] She was saying, "When she was young . . . she tried looking for the Grand High Witch."

TEACHER: Yes, Dale, but something happened at the beginning of that chapter that was sad. What was it?

DALE: [Hand up] Oooh, ooh, ooh. When his parents got killed.

TEACHER: That was sad, but that happened three chapters ago. Think about yesterday, Dale. What happened after the accident that made the boy and his grandmother sad?

DALE: The will!

72

TEACHER: Great! What was in the will?

[A long discussion about the will follows. Everyone takes part.]

TEACHER: Does anyone here speak another language?

DALE: Catchigadu, catchigadu. I speak Jamaican, man.

[Class laughs. Dale returns to his office! It is explained to him why he is sent there.]

October 22, 1988

[Teacher reads last paragraph from previous day's chapter to help pupils recall the events of the chapter. While teacher reads, Dale is throwing bits of eraser.]

TEACHER: [Stops reading] Would you like to stay with us and enjoy this chapter?

DALE: Yes.

TEACHER: Then you know what you should do.

[Dale stops throwing eraser and settles down to listen. Teacher continues with story.]

TEACHER: What are mussels?

DALE: [Hand up] Ooh, ooh.

TEACHER: Dale?

DALE: Kind of like oysters.

TEACHER: Good, Dale. Do you know anything else about them?

DALE: They're black.

TEACHER: Good, Dale. [Continues reading]

[Dale raises his hand quietly and waits for teacher to respond. This is the first time he has waited, so teacher stops reading to answer his request to speak.]

TEACHER: Yes, Dale.

DALE: My mother's boyfriend says that if I ate one he'd give me five bucks, but I didn't.

What struck me as important was that Dale waited his turn, shared this information, and felt a part of the story because he was the only one who knew what mussels were. It made him feel important and increased his self-esteem, if only for a short time. He settled down and the rest of the chapter was uneventful.

October 24, 1988

The book contains a chant that the Grand High Witch uses to warn her subjects of the consequences of disobedience. The class enjoyed the chant so much they asked if they could learn it. I wrote it on the blackboard, repeating each word as I wrote. The chant was fairly long, and we kept repeating it as I erased

73

one or two words at a time until the whole chant was erased except for the first word in each line.

All the children, overjoyed by their success, took turns reciting the chant. For some this was the first "memory work" they had learned, and repeating it was a risk they seldom took.

Dale was the last to volunteer. He kept repeating, "I can't do it." But the class repeated it with him a few times and helped him until he could do it completely by himself. He was *very* happy.

This success marked a milestone for Dale. He felt so good about himself that he shared the chant with all who would listen, building his self-esteem in the process.

The remainder of the book was completed with my goals for Dale achieved. He settled in to listen, waited his turn, and raised his hand, respecting the rights of others to be heard. There were times when he "forgot" and had to go to "the office", but during story time, these lapses were quite rare. In short, he learned to sit and listen, remember and share information in a positive successful way.

During the rest of the year we completed other novels without negative responses from Dale.

Dale still has difficulties in the school yard but has shown great improvement with this positive approach. On one occasion he actually told me, "I like it when you tell me what I should do, because then I know when I forget sometimes."

There is an epilogue to this story.

June 21, 1989
Conversation between Dale and Andrew regarding some school work.

> ANDREW: I'll let you beat me!
> DALE: It doesn't matter, it's not a race, Andrew!

Months before, Andrew wouldn't have let Dale beat him and Dale would have argued that he could beat Andrew anyway. Both these boys had gained self-esteem, and most importantly, they were sharing it!

It wasn't *only* talk that brought Dale out: it was also banishment from the possibility of taking part in talk — banishment to "the office". But above all, I am convinced that it was the seductiveness of talk, the fun and sharing that come with it, that changed his behavior and that of others in the class.

Current Events as a Springboard for Talk and Drama

BEVERLEY PHILIPS

Current events have always been a part of my classroom program. As far back as the sixties, when I was a raw teacher in a country town in New Zealand, I began each day with "news", as I called it then. Since that time, while teaching in Perth, Western Australia, inner-city schools in Toronto, and now in Peel, current events have continued to be a focus for me.

Thus, when musing about a suitable (and interesting, to me) research topic that focused on talk, "Current Events" seemed to be staring me in the face. My daily program was already in place. Indeed, since I teach a primary enhanced learning class and had "kept" ten students from the previous school year, I was amused and gratified that on the first day back at school last September, several of these children arrived with clippings of current news stories to discuss. My planned introduction to the new year was immediately scrapped!

Exploration

Having decided on the topic of my research inquiry I then had to find a focus. This took at least two months. I thought at first I would look at the way discussion of current events helps promote higher levels of thinking in gifted children. However, this seemed too obvious. I felt, too, that *all* children benefit from daily talking about news events. Finally, though, I decided on my focus: "Non-Fiction Reading and Talk of Gifted Children in the Primary Years". What a relief to have finally narrowed down my thoughts into a model I felt comfortable with!

Now I needed to research current literature. Since I had decided to use drama as the students' presentation vehicle I first read books and articles relating to learning, talk, and drama. Unfortunately, I was unable to find any literature specifically relating to non-fiction reading of young children, so any observations made in that area are without any backing but my own.

Method

My class, which comprises students from Grade One to Grade Three, is divided into three groups of six or seven taken from all grades. Each day they choose stories they want to present in dramatic form and how they want to present them (preparation); present them to the class; and undergo an evaluation, oral or written, afterwards. Each group presents one story a day.

During the course of this study, I videotaped talk in three phases: preparation, presentation, and evaluation. I realize that within these three main headings, there are many subtopics. However these were the focus of my observations. I have six videos of the talk which took place during the preparation, presentation, and evaluation sessions of each group and have included excerpts of transcripts which are most interesting and meaningful to me.

Transcripts

I found it very difficult to transcribe thoroughly, as there was always a lot of talk during the preparation times, and lots of "non-verbal" talk (gesturing and miming) during the earlier presentations. The evaluation sessions were easiest to record, since they tended to be more structured and full of talk.

Excerpt 1

Project coordinator Carol Thornley-Hall was present during a taped session when Group One discussed our process for using current events.

MRS. PHILIPS: What have we been doing with our current events?

JENA: We bring in things from newspapers.

MRS. P: How do you decide which events to present?

JAMES: We see whether they're easy or good or hard.

MRS. P: Do you mean easy to read?

MICHAEL: No, easy to act. We put them in piles and see what's best to do.

MRS. P: What happens if you can't read the paper — though I know you are all good readers!

MEREDITH: Big problem!

MRS. P: Could you solve that problem?

MEREDITH: Yes. Ask someone else.

CHRIS: You could decide not to do it!

76

MRS. P: That would really solve the problem! Does it really matter [if you can't read the piece]?

JAMES: Yes. You need lots of information.

MICHAEL: You need background information.

MRS. P: Back to my question. How do you decide which [events] to do?

JENA: We voted.

MEREDITH: We talked about them and then we voted.

MRS. T-H: Is some news more important than others?

MRS. P: Would you explain to Mrs. Thornley-Hall what kinds of news we have?

JAMES: International, which is all around the world; national, which is all of Canada; local, which is Toronto and Mississauga.

MRS. T-H: Is there any one of those which you use most often?

MICHAEL: Yes, international.

MRS. T-H: International?

MEREDITH: Yes — there's only a little bit of land that is local and national. So most is international.

MRS. P: Actually, Group One had one of each — local, national, and international, but that was just a coincidence, wasn't it?

JAMES: It was Newsgroup Three!

I was pleased that these students could explain the process we were using so well.

Excerpt 2: Preparation Talk

The following are sample comments made during all six preparation sessions. The students were already familiar with the events from which they had to choose, since they had been presented during our daily sharing time.

Note: these are snippets only and do not follow in any particular order.

M: You guys, it might be a good current event, but we have to think about how we are going to do it.

J: Let's read the article first and find out what really happened.

M: Who wants to do the architect one?

G: What's an architect anyway?

J: It means people who build things.

D: No, they draw.

G: Oh, now I understand.

M: How will we do it?

N: This one is about a peanut allergy.

D: I think we should do that one.

J: Especially me — since I'm in this group. [Puts the cutting on the "yes" pile] I have a lot of experience with that!

D: Who wants to do the one about the toy?

K: No!

D: That would be good.

K: All right.

M: You guys — how could we do this?

J: You could have a baby with an imaginary toy in his mouth.

M: Chris could be the baby. [Points to the youngest and smallest member of the group]

M: Then we could have the mother marching into Toys R Us.

J: Someone could be the Toys R Us guy — that would be hard.

D: That would be only three people.

M: But we could add other people.

D: Yes — the manager and the cashier and everyone else could be shoppers.

M: Okay. Who wants to do it? [All hands go up]

Excerpt 3: Presentation Talk

PILOT: Passengers — please buckle your seatbelts. We'll be leaving the terminal in one minute.

STEWARDESS: [moves down the aisle] Coloring books, anyone? Headphones one dollar each. Would you like a headphone, sir? [Plane sounds]

STEWARDESS: Coffee, tea, juice, or milk. What would you like? [Passengers answer] There you go.

PILOT: Passengers, please buckle your seatbelts, we're coming in for landing. . . We have come to a final stop.

STEWARDESS: Please exit by the exit doors. I hope you enjoyed your flight.
[Passengers leave]

PILOT: Hey, look! What's that there by the wheels? [Two figures crouch nearby]

STEWARDESS: It looks like two people — they must be frozen.

PILOT: Hey, are you okay?

STEWARDESS: We'd better call the ambulance. . .

This presentation of a story about two Trinidadian stowaways aboard a plane contained much more elaboration about events on the plane than did the original clipping. I was pleased with the way the group dramatized the news event and found the dialogue interesting and meaningful. This presentation had far more talk than the group's first effort.

Excerpt 4: Evaluation Talk

In the evaluations, I was mainly interested in hearing feelings and reflections, and all students were asked for their honest opinions. Peer evaluations were held immediately following each presentation; group evaluations — led by me and fairly structured — were made after each group viewed videotapes of its preparation and presentation.

PEER EVALUATIONS

Q = Question
C = Comment
A = Answer (by any group members)

C: With the stowaways, you could have added that they were smoking.
A: We were going to do that but they denied they were smoking.

Q: What gave you the ideas for the things the stewardess said?
A: I don't know — I've been on a lot of planes.

Q: Why were your presentations long?
A: Well, that's all we could do with them.

Q: Was it hard to get everyone to act?
A: [by the group leader] I had to yell at them a few times!

Q: How did you like being leader?
A: It was sort of tricky when Neil was being silly.
Q: How did you deal with that?
A: I just told him I would send him back to class.

GROUP EVALUATIONS

MRS. P: Do you think you learned anything by acting the current events?
JAMES: Yes we did.
MRS. P: What did you learn?
DANIEL: It's hard to put in the little details. It wasn't easy to do it without props.

JENA: I think it was hard for our group being first — Group Three was very good.
MRS. P: It was hard, but your group is next. That gives you a chance to improve.

Observations

I was disappointed that at first the actual presentations themselves produced the least amount of talk — "presentation" or "rehearsed" talk. The students seemed more intent on producing actions and sound effects (police sirens were popular!) to dramatize their stories and during the first round of presentations seemed reluctant to talk in case they gave too many clues to the audience about the topic. (At no time did I mention a competition or the need for mystery — I was always interested in the dialogue and interpretation of the current event in question, so it puzzles me that the students automatically thought this was to be a test. Perhaps it is a sign of their giftedness.) But after they watched and discussed videos of themselves, they changed their emphasis.

During the preparation sessions much talk was evident, all of it facilitated by the current events being discussed. There was a lot of arguing, problem-solving, and decision-making as well as social talk. But somehow each group was always able to reach a consensus about their three chosen pieces. I was pleased that all the leaders shown in the videos were able to problem-solve, allow for democratic decision-making, and encourage the more reluctant students to participate. It was exciting to hear discussions on world, national, and local events by such young children, and listen to the reasons the students gave as to whether or not a particular piece would make a good presentation. The presentations allowed for audience participation, questions, and "constructive" criticism. I was intent on involving the *whole* class and on several occasions suggested to the leaders that they ask the opinions of those who were saying little.

As I have already noted, each group's first presentation contained lots of action but very little talk. However, there was much change during later presentations, after we had viewed the initial tapes and the students saw for themselves how little conversation there was.

In the evaluation process, the whole class watched the videos of the presentations; then the group concerned watched its own presentation; and finally each group's final thoughts and reflections on its presentation were recorded. I led the discussions as I really wanted the sessions to be reflective, self-evaluative, and group-evaluative, and young children need guidance in these areas. I feel the transcripts show much insight.

After a few weeks I gave up on audiotaping the daily current events presentations. It was just too time-consuming to tape and transcribe every day. Instead, I carefully made notes in my journal of the daily topics and any interesting discussions that ensued. I was particularly interested to note the progress in the talk of the two or three students in the class who began the year being very non-communicative. One boy, Kevin, began bringing in current events daily last October and has not missed a day since. At first we were barely able to hear him, but now his confidence has grown and he is always most eager to share. His pieces are always very interesting and not merely "fluff" items. (His parents obviously help him, as often certain paragraphs or sentences in his clippings have been highlighted, but I feel this is an advantage for us all.)

When preparing this paper, which I have shared with my students, I orally read through the list of topics in my journal, to see if they had any memory of the items. Guess what? They remember more than I do!

The following are random questions and answers that have occurred to me during the process of my inquiry.

Q: How many children were involved in each day's reporting of current events?
A: A glance through my journal shows a high of twelve and a low of four. This does not include those who were involved in questions and comments following each piece.

Q: Did current events help affective development?
A: Yes, particularly for the more reluctant talkers who are now quite comfortable reporting, questioning, presenting, and evaluating (in talk and in writing). All students have had the opportunity to lead and present in front of the class and guests.

Q: How about cognitive learning?
A: I truly believe that by using current events in this way, the students have broadened their general knowledge and through our talk have been led to think about world, national, and local issues. Romania, the Berlin Wall, and

Lithuania, to name but a few subjects, now have real meaning to these young students. In terms of non-fiction reading, the way our scrapbooks and class book (both containing records of subjects we have covered) are grabbed during daily individual reading time surely indicates that the children's reading vocabulary has been expanded too, though time restraints and a loathing on my part for word tests, result in no actual evidence. Geography skills have also increased, and the children love poring over the world map on the wall of our classroom.

Q: How important were the videos?

A: They became the focal point of my inquiry — for the students as well as for me. By viewing them, the children found out that some of their initial questions and comments during evaluation were unkind, and they learned to rephrase their thoughts. It was relatively easy to reach a group consensus in evaluation, once the tapes were viewed — they could see the results of their talk. (Many of the parents have borrowed the tapes for home viewing, so obviously the children talk all this out at home too!)

When viewing the videos, I felt initially that I was talking too much. Now I think that much of what I was saying supported what had already taken place and offered guidance — particularly after the initial drama acts, when not much talk occurred. We reviewed role-playing, use of tableaux, use of narrators, the relevance of mime, and so on. (And as David Booth says, "You need adult intervention to have deep learning.")

Q: Are current events a useful vehicle for promoting talk with and between primary students?

A: The answer, of course, has to be "yes", particularly if an effort is made to involve all children — not just the *one* child presenting his or her piece with no follow-up questions, comments, or reflections.

Q: Was there need for a structure in the process of the inquiry?

A: Yes, particularly when it came to the drama components. Young children do not always present drama in an effective way and I did not want the presentations to be mindless skits which evoked laughter from the audience but little else.

82

Q: Does the word "gifted" need to be included in my inquiry title?

A: Yes and no. I feel that the process I have used could be successful with any class — all children are capable of talking about current events. Howver, the non-verbal reading component may be more difficult for younger "average" primary children; perhaps headlines only could be used, or other modifications made.

Conclusion

I have enjoyed my year working on this inquiry and really examining for the first time why and how I use current events in my program. I believe that, given enthusiasm on the part of the teacher, a genuine desire to enrich and expand children's minds in terms of their oral language, reading, and writing development, current events can become a wonderfully exciting vehicle which can be used in any classroom, at any level, and most importantly with children of any intellectual ability. The results may astound you.

4. Drama as a Way of Learning: The Role of Talk in Dramatic Activity

Drama presents children with an added dimension in the talk curriculum — the power of speaking and listening while in role. Children at play understand this mode of expression, and easily slip into and out of role at the dress-up centre, playing with blocks, or building towns in the sandbox. Opportunities for exploring the medium of talk occur as children engage in more structured dramatic play, dramatizing a story, working through a simulation activity, or creating a scene such as depicting the arrival of new immigrants to North America. In dramatic learning, children can try on different language patterns, speaking formally as, for instance, the governor of a land challenging an unfair ruler, debating an issue with an interplanetary council, or reading aloud a proclamation they have written. Because much of drama is a "living through" experience, the heat of the moment demands children listen and respond in authentic ways, controlling the direction and outcome of the work from within. Drama talk can be a powerful means of assisting children in using talk to communicate and reflect.

In her Grade Two classroom, for instance, Leann Oswald presents a variety of activities for the children to choose from. Her inquiry focused on the puppet theatre. She was interested in the variations in work from rehearsal to performance. The children enjoyed dramatizing situations, problems, or incidents, but had difficulty in re-enacting their rehearsals in front of a group. As her inquiry continued, the interest level in the puppet theatre decreased, and the children were hesitant to rehearse and perform for fear of evaluation. Leann concluded that the children were unwilling or unable to sustain their playtalk during performance, due to the pressure of the audience, and in order to keep the activity creative and spontaneous, the children involved with the puppets should be allowed to see the sharing of their ideas not as a rigid rehearsed performance, but

84

as an opportunity to create a puppet play through the spontaneous flow of ideas in improvisation.

In her level three classroom, Sue-Anne Gyles worked with a picture book in drama, and videotaped the children discussing their efforts at creating a village tapestry they had heard about in the story. Their responses at being told it was now enchanted demonstrated their involvement in the imaginary situation. They began to pose questions and problems, working with partners, in small groups, and as a whole class, coming to grips with the issues that grew from the drama and becoming absorbed in their work. As one child wrote in her journal, "When we watched the tape the teacher made of us, it felt like ten minutes but it took an hour."

Carol Cameron decided to examine Brian Cambourne's conditions for learning — immersion, demonstration, expectation, responsibility, approximation, employment, and feedback — and how they could facilitate learning through drama. She recorded her experiences with a class as they built drama from a picture book, developing the scenario through role play and improvisation. Her collaborative learning adventure uncovered opportunities for problem-solving, exploring writing skills, and reading and creative arts activities. The children unveiled themselves, their interests, and their values through their drama experiences.

As the following papers show, drama can involve extremely lively talk and engagement.

Storytelling with Junior Kindergarten Children

CAROLYN DAVIS

Drama may be the most effective means of providing children with experiences of different types of speaking and listening. With this in mind, I focused my attention on storytelling to Junior Kindergarten children, and followed up by observing them as they mimicked these stories.

Storytelling is easy to promote when there is a connection to play. As I observed the children's play, I realized stories provide ideas and stimuli for play. In my readings, I discovered three factors necessary to help children reach their language potential vis à vis stories:

1. storytelling by an enthusiastic storyteller;

2. opportunities for imaginative play;
3. an environment in which a child can have a variety of language experiences.

With a large percentage of ESL children in my class, I chose exciting, imaginative, short stories with large descriptive pictures. I made extensive use of a flannel board and puppets to enhance the stories.

I decided to concentrate on the version of the story "The Three Billy Goats Gruff" by Paul Caldone because the language he uses is predictable and patterned, and it is a story about a scary character. After reading the story I left the book in an accessible place, and a few children looked at it. Then I retold the story using flannel board props. Much to my delight, as I started to tell the story the children spontaneously joined in and soon they were all chanting, "Trip, Trap, Trip, Trap", first softly and then louder, as I told them about the gaots going across the bridge. I had been the storyteller; now the children wanted to be part of the dialogue. They had listened well.

The flannel board props were available for the children's play, and the children used them well. Standing back and listening I realized they were in control, moving the props around on the flannel board and using their imaginations, making inferences and predictions.

A few weeks later we went for a walk to a nearby creek, and much to the children's surprise we came to a bridge over the creek. The children were concerned that the troll in the story might live there. Of course we acted out the story. Several children wanted to be the troll. I wanted the performance to be a success, so I chose Billy, who was an imaginative, curious, extremely capable actor. The children decided a small child should be the littlest Billy Goat, an average child the second brother, and a big child the biggest goat. So they followed the sequential development of the story. The four actors became the characters in the story and the other children enthusiastically contributed with "Trip, Trap". The actors made up their own dialogue and the flow of the story continued. At the end of the production the audience applauded and wanted to hear the play again. The second performance was not as successful. Boredom was already setting in, and the four new actors were not as imaginative as the first group. We ended the play quickly and then looked under the bridge for the troll. The children predicted he was "hiding in the woods" or "under the school". Places were mentioned that were meant to haunt us for the remainder of the day.

Upon our arrival back at the school, our walk in the woods led to fantasy play in the Home and Block centres. Only one boy went to the Home Centre, where he tried unsuccessfully to initiate a re-enactment of the story. The girls wanted to play house. Thereafter interest waned.

Earlier in the school year we enjoyed the chant "Going on a Bear Hunt". The actions, rhythm, repetition, and patterning gave the ESL children an opportunity to participate while playing with language. Using pictures as props, all the children recited the chant together. At activity times a few children repeated the chant to each other although they did not follow the sequence of events. Several weeks later, I observed two children listening to a tape of "The Bear Hunt". This would have gone unnoticed except that I heard a voice I had never heard before. Quietly standing in the background, I listened to Trang recite "The Bear Hunt" in English. Until that day I had never heard Trang speak English, nor did I think she understood the language. I now realize she had mastered the English language but hadn't felt confident to speak until this non-threatening situation.

In my Junior Kindergarten room I now have props to enhance language acquisition for the ESL child. My research confirmed that children demonstrate comprehension by dramatizing stories.

Dramatic Play in Grade One
EVELYN BRUNO

The Beginning

Frustration is the word that comes to mind when describing my early involvement in the TALK Project. It sounded very new and exciting, especially the emphasis on our role as researchers and inquirers. But what was I to inquire about? Very few guidelines were given and, as a result, many of us experienced some panic. Up until now, teachers were used to getting things "handed down from above". I myself kept looking for some magic idea or question that I could answer about children's talk. But over time, I became more and more focused on what was going on in my own classroom. Yes, my students were talking! Over a period of several months, I became more aware of and interested in patterns of play and talk that were developing in my Grade One class. This was the beginning. . .

The Inquiry

In my play-based program, a great deal of time is spent sharing a variety of good literature — fairy tales, chants, poems, songs, and stories based on a particular theme or unit of study. I have also begun to have "Book Talks" with the class, and use many of Aidan Chambers' ideas to get children talking and responding to books. During play time, or "Exploration Time", as I called it, groups of children often created their own versions of the stories or chants they had learned. They would spend days and even weeks creating and re-creating favorite stories in their spontaneous play. In my role as observer and listener, I became very interested in the talk and complex interactions that took place during these dramatic play episodes. I had always believed in the value of spontaneous play for learning but questioned its role in the development of specific skills. I discovered that by listening to, and documenting, and analysing childrens' play talk, I could begin to gain a better understanding of the role it has in learning.

The Data

Collecting data on videotape proved to be an enjoyable yet sometimes frustrating experience. Some days I felt like a technical expert behind the camera, but on other days, things just didn't work out the way they were supposed to. In addition, the dramatic play was so spontaneous that I was not always prepared to capture exciting moments on tape. The children certainly liked being filmed, however, and often hammed it up for the camera.

Throughout the year, I collected a variety of audio and video data of children playing, of group discussions, and of children talking about the importance of play and talk.

The Discoveries

From my observation of the data collected, I discovered that dramatic play provides children with the opportunity to practise and develop a variety of skills. I also found that there are different types of talk which serve different purposes or functions. These functions are illustrated in the following diagram:

FUNCTIONS OF PLAY TALK

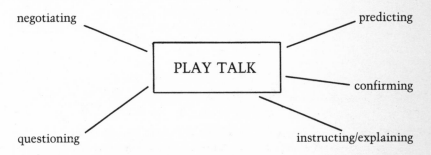

These represent only some of the functions of children's talk; more may be revealed in other forms of play. For my purposes however, I will focus on these five: instructing, questioning, negotiating, confirming, and predicting.

The Talk

As part of a theme called "All Kinds of Structures", my class shared many versions of "The Three Little Pigs". The children discussed their likes and dislikes, as well as questions they had and patterns discovered in each version. One day, a group of children began planning a play of their version of the story, which they called "The Three Little Pigs and the Wicked Witch". Much of their play time was spent preparing for the drama. I found this preparation stage to be evident in all of the dramatic play episodes I observed. During this stage, the children busily set up props, negotiated roles, discussed storyline, and created costumes. The following transcription is an example of this preparation stage:

> [A group of children are standing around a table with glue, scissors, and paper. They are wearing paper pig hats and pigs' tails.]

A: Can someone cut me a piece of tape?

C1: Can you make a moustache and a tophat? [talking to David, who is playing the man selling bricks]

C2: What color bow tie do you want?

D: Black.

A: No, black and grey.

C1: What else do you need? [she holds paper moustache up to David]   [questioning]

D: I'm going to look stupid in it.

C1: No you won't. . . I'm going to twirl it. . . remember like the old guys with the twirl at the end?   [confirming]

A: Uh huh, this is what I think, I think it should be like this. [Andrea folds a piece of paper]   [explaining]

C: Cora, you know when you're doing the bricks [building the brick house], pretend that you're putting on cement. [Connie moves her hand back and forth like a trowel]
                                                [instructing]

C1: Okay, that's what I'll do.

E: I need to make something.

C: Then make it.

A: I'm going to make a new pig nose, you know why? I don't like the other one.

C1: Here's your moustache. [hands it to David]

E: What about a beard? We can make a beard too.

C2: Is that your beard? [David holds a piece of black paper up to his chin]   [questioning]

D: Yeah.

C2: Good.

E: Cora, do you wanna be a boy or a girl?   [questioning]

C1: I'm a girl pig, *everyone* is a girl pig.   [confirming]

A: No, we should make him young like this. . . [Andrea draws beard]

D: I know, a young boy. . .

C1: I know, but they have moustaches too.

E: Yeah, my Dad has a moutache. . .   **[confirming]**

C2: [to Andrea] Don't forget to take off your pig's tail when you become a witch.   **[instructing]**

C2: [to all] We have to work hard everybody or it will take too long.   **[predicting]**

C1: Go get in your places.

A: [to Cora] No, some people are not done.

C1: You don't have to shout at me   **[negotiating]**

A: I wasn't shouting.

C1: Okay, places everyone. . .

E: I'm the bricks, remember?

C1: No, I'm the bricks, it's like before.

E: Cora, you always want to be bricks. BRICKS! BRICKS! BRICKS!

C1: Well anyways, don't you want to come to my house first. . . I mean to my house last. PLEASE!   **[negotiating]**

E: I'll be baby?

C1: Okay, you can be the little baby and I'm the bricks.
    [negotiating]

E: I'll be only one week old. . . I'm only one week old.

C1: I know . . . places.

C2: Places everybody.

Analysis of the Play Talk

A great deal of language and thinking must take place in order for children to construct and coordinate meaning in a shared dramatic play context. The preceding transcripts reveal the different functions of play talk as the children speak and act spontaneously. The talk facilitates the development of important skills. Spontaneous play calls upon children to practise communication skills and thereby develop greater confidence in their abilities to use language. It provides a medium in which problems may be identified, investigated, and solved by children. Practice is gained in self-discipline and cooperation with others. Children establish an imaginary world and develop their sense of story through talk. The groups of children I observed worked hard to create and sustain their plays. This commitment to task was fascinating.

Extensions of Play

Play itself is a valuable and worthwhile activity, but it also provides a basis for additional learning activities. This group of children, for example, later decided to create a "rap" about their version of the story of the three pigs. Other spin-offs that evolved from the play were big books, tapes, and published stories. These were shared with the class and with others and enjoyed by all.

Conclusion

Carol Thornley-Hall says that "talk is the keyhole to children's minds". By listening to children's talk, teachers will be better able to meet their students' individual needs. And by providing a variety of opportunities for play talk, we can facilitate the development of important skills.

I hope to continue this inquiry in the fall and plan to apply the knowledge I have gained to more structured drama activities. I am also curious about the role of play and talk in the development of reading and writing skills.

Gordon Wells states in his book, *The Meaning Makers*, that teachers should become their own "theory builders" and base their theories on what they are practising. My inquiry has enabled me to do this. The process has been meaningful — the talking, listening, collaborating, arguing, reading, and writing have developed my skills as observer, listener, and facilitator. I believe that I have "enacted" the curriculum through my inquiry, and as a result, I have become a more effective learner and educator.

5. Talk and the ESL Child

Children new to the English language have already acquired the ability to speak and listen as they interact, but only in their own mother tongue. The obstacles that arise as they enter a new language culture are not only those of becoming familiar with English, but also of the risks involved in taking part in classroom activities, being members of a group, using language as a medium for learning, and learning to control their words for maximum effect. Children learning to speak English need the security of an environment that both supports and contributes to their beginning efforts, so that the classroom becomes a place where talk is nurtured, enabling the children to risk and grow.

Teachers of ESL children are developing powerful strategies and techniques for helping their students participate in classroom activities in which language facility grows from their interest in and commitment to learning events.

For her talk inquiry, Ann Halo researched factors affecting second language acquisition in order to assist ESL students in developing their communication skills. She focused on one young girl, and developed activities in a small group setting, with encouragement and a non-threatening environment to reduce anxiety and allow for risk-taking. Through pair work, peer tutoring, role-playing, interviews, and collaborative learning, the student increased the time she spent on communicative language activities, improving the quality and quantity of conversation. A case study such as Ann's demonstrates the learning a teacher can acquire in examining one child's progress over a period of time.

The library became the centre of Lois McMurray's study of her ESL children, in an attempt to empower them with strategies for succeeding in school. In the past, the Bookmobile had called at the school, but since this service had been withdrawn, Lois, remembering an incident in the previous year of a refugee parent's frustration in trying to secure a library card, set up visits to the library branch closest to the school. Prior to the first visit, applications for cards were filled out and general information sessions were held. This was followed with an orientation day at the library, and then visits every three weeks. Children took out books in English and in their mother tongues, and on the final visit, a summer reading program was discussed. Lois concluded that talk was important in enhancing the impact of the public library on the lives and the language of the children, the ownership the children felt in choosing books and cassettes, and the interest of parents in seeing the community as a resource.

Susan Francescini decided to examine the role of talk in the cooperative writing of Grade Two ESL/ESD students who had not acquired oral proficiency but who were attempting to develop their reading and writing skills. She used a series of activities based on cooperative group writing because it requires talk. A comparison was drawn between the amount of talk occurring during the writing process and the quality of text produced by each group. Susan concluded that ESL/ESD students require more student talk as part of the pre-writing and writing activities, benefiting from oral discussion and sharing of ideas and experiences in relaxed, non-threatening small group sessions. Children need to write and talk as part of the same activity, often simultaneously.

Other teachers examined different aspects of communicating with ESL children, as the following papers show.

The Role of Personality in the Acquisition of a Second Language

SHELLEY KATZ

In my Junior Kindergarten classes, it is not unusual to find children who arrive at school speaking no English. These children, from diverse ethnic backgrounds, usually have not spent any time with people other than their immediate and extended families. This year I chose to study two such children — Shelton and Alexander. Shelton is a large boy from Hong Kong; Alexander is slim, average in height, and also from Hong Kong. They both speak Cantonese at home.

94

Shelton entered the class in the fall with interest, but he did not show much emotion. His mother stayed for part of the first morning and then left. He didn't appear upset, but he did attempt to climb out the window after her. When we retrieved him my assistant sat with him. It became clear that he was upset, but he remained very quiet, covering up all his emotions. He seemed more angry than sad. As I came to know Shelton better, I found that he seemed to understand simple instructions, but I soon realized he was reading my gestures more than understanding my words. Early on in our relationship he exhibited a very stubborn, closed manner, both with the other children and with me. Shelton didn't really speak, but he did refuse, with his actions, to follow any rules or routines. He said "no" when he was asked to get off the climber at story or singing time. His mother was asked to speak to him, but it didn't do any good. At our first parents' night, his father asked him to promise that he would "listen to Mrs. Katz". Shelton's reply was, "I no listen to Mrs. Katz". Again his father made the request, and again Shelton refused. Several days later his mother came into the class and said that she had told Shelton that if he didn't listen to me, he wouldn't get any food. Since Shelton loves to eat, he did begin to obey orders, but still with much urging and reminding from both me and my assistant.

In November Shelton was still not really cooperative, and his English continued to be very sparse and weak. He hated songs and rhymes, and when we sang he often covered his ears and said, "I hate that song." He was listening to books being read aloud, but he seemed to hate anything in which he had to orally participate.

Shelton now speaks in very short sentences when playing near others, or talking to an adult. He says such things as, "It's a house", "It's a train", "I made a CN Tower". If asked a question, he answers in a very short sentence or phrase. I believe that his personality — his closed, stubborn approach to all situations — is making it more difficult for him to acquire fluency in English.

Alexander also entered our class with his mother, who told us he didn't speak any English at all. When she left, he cried openly, and for about a week, he would sit near the door of the room, crying. We asked an older child, who we thought spoke Cantonese, to sit with him. He hugged her but continued to cry. I learned how to say "Mommy will come back soon" in Cantonese, and that seemed to help a little. After several days his crying eased off, though it recurred from time to time. But even as Alexander cried, he was totally aware of what was happening around him, perhaps because of his open, receptive personality. As he was crying, he would still point out things that were lying on the floor or out of place. He seemed to know somehow what was amiss in the room, and what the children should be doing. As he was crying in his corner, he was noting the routines and actions of me, my assistant, and his classmates. Early on, he ventured into the centre of the room to get a tissue. He was a risk-taker from the beginning, which I think has facilitated his excellent acquisition of English.

By October 5 he had begun to repeat words I said while looking at books and small toys. On October 13, the curtains of the classroom were closed when he entered with his grandfather, and he immediately became upset and wanted them opened, perhaps so he could see his grandfather walking away and wave goodbye to him. This was a real setback; Alex cried all day, again sitting on his stool by the door. When he calmed down he sat with me and we looked at a book together. He repeated "bud", and said on his own "house", "butterfly", and "fish". Although I had assumed he was doing well in adjusting to school, I wondered — was his adjustment so frail that closed curtains could completely topple it?

On October 16, Alex went into the washroom, came out, and made a strange face. My assistant, Sharon, asked, "Is it a mess?" — and he nodded his head to say yes. The washroom *was* a mess and he was able to communicate that to us.

Alex began to gesture and mimic the active play of others, and they accepted him. Whenever we played together, he constantly made eye contact with me, perhaps for approval or for an explanation — I don't know.

By the last week of October, he was becoming much more sociable, and was being taken by others to the blocks centre or to the climber. The children seemed to like his quiet manner, his interested and smiling face. One day he went to the globe and I showed him China; he repeated "China". While playing with puzzles, he asked me, "What's this?" I answered, "A boy." He continued to ask "What's this?" about several puzzle pieces. He also said "stop" when looking at a stop sign. He spent his days playing with children on the climber, at big blocks, or at an animal matching game. All of the activities he chose involved social interaction with other children. On October 24, while playing at the duplo train with Katerina, he said, "It's a train." That was his first full sentence, and since then his English fluency has skyrocketed into very complex sentences.

On October 26, when I left the room he asked my assistant, "Where Katz go?" On October 27, he made a jack-o-lantern and gave it to me, saying "This for you" and "That is scary".

By early November, Alex seemed to understand almost all that was said to him. He continued to be very sociable and to play with almost all of the children in cooperative or associative play situations.

On November 14, after hearing the story *The Gingerbread Man*, Alex said "a cookie man" and "the cookie in the oven". During activity time he said, "Can I do the ball?" and, "Shelton is here." The next day he had his hair combed in a new, "cool" way, with gel. I asked him, "Who did your hair?" He replied, "My grandfather."

On November 22, Alexander came up to me during activity time, said "I know", and proceeded to re-enact the entire finger play *Open Them, Shut Them* exactly as I do it, until the very end and with all the correct actions.

One day in November Alex and Shelton were playing at small blocks. It was a unique opportunity to transcribe their conversation and to note the differences between their English.

ME: Who made this?
SHELTON: I did and Shelton made this.
ALEX: Don't break it.
ALEX: This is a CN Tower.
ME: [to Shelton] Did you make a CN Tower?
SHELTON: Yeah.
ME: Which one is taller?
ALEX: Me. [he's right]
ME: How did you hurt your head?
ALEX: Fall at my house.
SHELTON: We don't break it. [pointing to his tower]
ME: Uh oh, crash! [the tower falls over]
SHELTON: Yeah, crash.
ME: That's a rectangle. [picking up one block]
ALEX: A rectangle like a square.

ME: Yes, it's like a rectangle but the square is shorter. Which is the tallest tower?

SHELTON: This is a boat.

ME: Gee, that looks nice.

SHELTON: Yeah. [he is carefully taking a block from the middle, but the whole pile of blocks fall down.]

ME: Why does it fall?

SHELTON: [no answer] Oops.

ME: You used all the blocks.

SHELTON: Yeah — no more.

ALEX: I can make it. [He points to an illustration of a building on the block box. He keeps looking and tries to replicate the building.]

SHELTON: We have to tidy up. . . . Hey, we have it. [pointing to box]

ALEX: I do it. No. [he moves Shelton's hand]

Alex seemed to welcome the challenge of copying the block design, even if it was hard. Shelton wanted to tidy up, perhaps because he found the task too hard and felt frustrated.

As Alex became more fluent in English, his social activity in the room also increased. He was eager to play with others, both in the room and outside, and his English flourished. Shelton, on the other hand, remained very isolated, choosing to play by himself, only speaking when someone asked him something. As expected, his English did not improve much.

While watching Shelton and Alexander, I also thought about the personalities of other ESL children I have taught in my Junior Kindergarten class. The children who have had strong negative personalities, who were anti-social or demanded attention in negative ways, did not seem to acquire English as easily as those who were outgoing and interested in being socially accepted by their peers. The "closed" child who does not seek peer approval or inclusion is not warmly accepted into a group, and therefore does not acquire the fluency in English that the friendly child does. It's almost like a self-fulfilling prophecy — "I don't like them, I don't want to play," the child thinks. The group perceives him as "mean" or "bad", and they ignore him. His communication skills, which might help him, are used to indicate that he wishes to play alone. The result is that he remains alone and lacking in essential verbalization skills.

Shelton, for example, pouted, hid, ran away, and refused to obey for several weeks. I took this behavior to be an example of a hard, strong, disobedient child. When he relaxed and began to warm up to us, I realized he was a very sensitive, warm, caring child who kept all of his emotions under strict control. Shelton ultimately began to listen and came to love school, but he remained a loner, playing by himself or, sometimes, next to another child — rarely *with* others.

It is now May, and Shelton is communicating a little more fully, using short sentences, but conversing on a day-to-day basis. His pronunciation is poor; he omits many final consonant sounds. Alex speaks frequently, enjoys expressing his thoughts or observations, and is an avid participant in class conversations. He speaks in a quiet voice, but without an accent or speech irregularity.

If I am in the same school next year, I will be quite interested to see how Shelton and Alex fare in Senior Kindergarten. If I am not in the school in the coming year, perhaps I will have to visit the Senior Kindergarten class to see what the next stage of their fluency in English will bring.

Communication through Body Talk

RUTH ICHIYEN

As a Kindergarten ESL teacher, I work with children who have various degrees of English-language proficiency. The majority of students I come in contact with were born outside Canada and are hearing English in my classroom for the first time. However, several of my students were born in Canada but have little exposure to English as their parents speak only their native language at home. As a result, these students have only a limited knowledge of English, gained primarily from watching TV. Although hearing English in this way provides a starting point for learning the language, it is only through becoming more actively involved in speaking that a person begins to become proficient in it.

Such is the case of Suneil, my target for study in this TALK Project. Suneil, age five, came to Kindergarten having had little exposure to English. The language most commonly used in his home is Hindi. Through interviews with his mother, it has been determined that Suneil was late in learning to speak. He did not begin to talk until three and a half years of age and is not yet proficient in his native language, Hindi. Despite his language deficiencies, Suneil is a very bright, verbal, and confident child.

At the present time, Suneil is still learning the structure of the English language. His speech lacks the use of proper verb tenses and shows limited use of articles and prepositions. There is little subject/verb agreement in his sentences, and he misplaces many words and phrases. He cannot ask properly phrased questions.

Yet, despite these many obstacles which he has to overcome in English, Suneil is able to make himself understood the majority of the time through his creative use of body language. He enjoys storytelling, as he shows in the videotape segment which appears later in this paper, and is compensating for his lack of language proficiency with the use of body language and drama. Through this expressive form of "talk", his audience is able to decipher his speech and its meaning.

This has important implications for teachers of ESL as well as regular classroom teachers, for if a student is able to make himself better understood through body talk, so too can teachers make themselves better understood to their students using this physical form of communication. Jo Gusman, in her seminar, "ESL: Whole Language Strategies", held in Toronto in 1990, indicates that students remember only 7 percent of what they learn in a day, 35 percent if some facial expression was included in the presentation, and 58 percent if material was presented with expressive body language.

Body language, then, is clearly an important component of talk. ESL teachers need to both demonstrate and encourage the use of body language, so that students less exuberant than Suneil will also be willing to express themselves with this valuable aid to communication. Further, using body "talk" will also ensure that our messages will be more accurately interpreted and retained by students. For example, when teaching the concept of "hot" and "cold", the teacher could use body "talk" to depict these concepts. This would more firmly embed the meanings of these words. Similarly, when reading a story, acting out key sections would likely improve students' comprehension of the story.

The following transcript is taken from a sharing time in a kindergarten group. This is an example of how Suneil is unable to clearly communicate verbally, and yet through his body "talk", the others are able to better understand him.

Suneil had just been telling the group that he was going to get a new bike soon. By reading the transcript alone, it is difficult to determine what Suneil is saying. However, with the aid of the videotape, it becomes much clearer, primarily because of Suneil's extensive use of body language.

S = Suneil
T = Teacher
S1 = Student 1
S2 = Student 2

S: I'm going to get my bike too.
T: You're going to get a new bike too?
S: [nods]
T: Boy, you're lucky. I hope you can ride it.
S: [nods]
T: Do you think you can ride it?
S: Then I'm going to ride. [stands up] I can do [demonstration] fast as I can.
T: Oh you can. Have you ridden a bike before? No, so it will be your first time. I bet you'll be good at it, Suneil.
S: My mom going to buy me new toy Batman. Batman, I going to get — Batman gun. [demonstration]
T: A Batman gun?
S: [stands up] Yeah, there it is — a gun. [stands up and draws it in the air] Jit, jit, jit.
S1: It's a water gun?
S: No.
S2: A movie camera?
S: No.
S2: Yeah.
S: Toy gun! [demonstration]
T: It's a toy gun [Suneil laughs] so it's not going to hurt anyone. Right, Suneil?
S: That is toy — no gun stuff. [shows with hands]
T: Nothing.
S1: Just noises come?
S: No, just you press this [demonstration], and I going to get Superman.
T: You're going to get Superman too?
S: And ring.
S1: And Penguin?
S: Penguin, yeah — I see tomorrow Superhero.

101

T: Uh huh.

S: And there's toy and and Robin shut [i.e., shot]. [demonstration] Mr. Freeze friend he get —

S1: It's not Mr. Freeze friend. This is Superman ring.

S: Get then Robin, shut [i.e., shoot]. [demonstration] He shoot um for . . . He shut —

S1: Superman dead?

S: No — the ring for Mr. Freeze, he get shot down then Penguin was shoot and Superman fall down.

T: Uh huh.

S: And I saw Superman TV and boy walking, and and that man and and lady said you want some serikat [sic]? Then Superman and lady get for him. [demonstration] And what Superman said? Don't worry that shrunk and he come in school. . . boy. I saw that TV.

T: You saw that on TV. When did you see that on TV? Yesterday, Suneil, when you got home last night?

S: I see tomorrow, Monday, yesterday.

T: Monday was yesterday.

S: Thundercats.

T: Thundercats, boy you watch a lot of TV, Suneil, don't you?

S: And Thundercats there is lying. [stands up]

S1: Your mom's going to buy you Nintendo?

S: [ignores S1] And he choo choo and he fall down [falls down himself] and lady and I see He-Man movie, TV — movie some, and He-Man [stands up and demonstrates] is trying [demonstration] and they two He-Man is. . .

S1: Not two He-Man — it's a skeleton and he's a He-Man.

S: Two He-Man is . . . try stretch. I saw Monday . . . when he's twenty-five and he stretch and then he . . . ATCHOO [pretends to sneeze] — nother one get out and he got the small one. He did ATCHOO [pretends to sneeze], then he say SHH and he [demonstration] going. He had no eyes 'cause he blind and and I. . .

T: It's just as good as a movie — just watching you, Suneil.

Talk between Buddies

KATHLEEN LEWIS

My involvement in the TALK Project led me to explore the role of talk between an ESL child and an English-speaking child in a writing situation. This was of interest to me as I had a great number of ESL children in my classroom. How would a child develop in the use of the English language? What were the best strategies that a teacher could provide for acquiring English, and how? How would the use of English in talk progress into writing and reading in the English language?

By pairing an ESL child with an English-speaking child, it was my belief that the latter would offer the former a good role model and would play an important part in the ESL child's acquisition of English. Language input must precede language output. By buddying up with another child, an ESL learner can utilize a friend's linguistic skills as needed input.

Deanna is an example of a Grade One ESL child who used her friend this way in a learning situation. Deanna was born in Yugoslavia, the first child of well-educated, caring parents who immigrated to Canada six months ago. The Serbian language was spoken in the home, with a little English. Deanna had attended the last term of Kindergarten in a school here, and her school records showed a somewhat aggressive personality and behavior. Upon entering our classroom, she appeared rather a shy, quiet child who sat alone, without attempting to join other children at play or when given a task to complete. She was left to observe the other children, to join them when she felt comfortable.

Within the first few days, she was able to draw a picture and to tell me about it. At this point she chose to play with another little girl, Sharon. This relationship was encouraged and a friendship began. The puppet stage was often their choice as a place to meet and role-play. Changes in Deanna's attitude began to be apparent. During free exploration times she shared activities and talk with Sharon. At writing time they sat together, and the ESL child was able to observe the writing process. Questions were asked and answered, help was given, and growth began to happen.

In the conversation below, both girls were working on their own tasks:

D: Sharon, how do you spell "we"?
S: W-e. Nothing else.
D: All w-e.
S: That's all.
D: We are . . . are?
S: Sound it out. [puts hand on Deanna's shoulder]
D: How about do I sound it out?

103

s: That's easy. We are: a-r-e.
D: We a-r-e. We are playing.
s: A game. We are playing.
D: Play. [she tries to sound it out] P-i.
s: Play.
D: How do you sepll "l"?
s: A stick, stick, stick, stick. A-y.
D: -y -y. How do you spell "y"? How do I spell "y"?

[Both girls look at the alphabet cards at the front of the class-room and recite the alphabet to y.]

Shortly after this conversation, Sharon's first book, *About Friends* was published. It was dedicated to Deanna, who now seemed to feel very much a part of our classroom. She was happy. She remained on task, determined to publish her own book. She took risks in her writing and shared her achievements. Her self-confidence grew, as did her self-esteem. I saw her engaged with Sharon in social talk and talk for learning. They were sharing an experience of friendship and making use of each other's strengths. Deanna was remarkably successful in her conversations with Sharon in getting help with writing. She got her attention by often using her name, touching her, and making specific requests of her. She obviously wanted to learn.

One-to-one interaction is a significant factor in the acquisition of language. Through buddying, a child can come to feel comfortable and know that his or her contributions are valid. I believe that my inquiry clearly shows the importance of a good role model for the ESL child, and indicates that friendship plays a most positive role in the learning process.

Epilogue

Reflections on the Talk Curriculum

DAVE RIDDELL

Over the past two years, I have had the experience of participating in the TALK Project at two different levels. I was involved as a classroom teacher in the initial year, and as an acting vice-principal of one of the project schools in the second year. Although these two involvements have overlapped considerably, I still find them distinct in the perspectives they offered me on the project. It is with these experiences behind me that I want to share some of my observations and reflections.

As a teacher sitting in on the first full professional activity day in September 1988, I recall listening carefully to David Booth, Gordon Wells, Sar Khan, and Carol Thornley-Hall outline their views of what the project held for us. Upon leaving, several of my colleagues and I were confused as to what the focus of the project was and what expectations the administration had in mind when it came to our commitment. The in-school workshops that followed in the next few weeks did little to clear up my confusion over this matter. The only real item that kept coming forth at these sessions was that of classroom research, or more specifically, classroom observation. At every professional development session for the TALK Project, I came away with the idea of taking an aspect of my classroom program (problem-solving in math, science experiments, discussion groups in reading, etc.) and studying it. How I was going to do this and in what area were the ongoing questions that troubled me throughout my initial involvement in the project. At this point of confusion and worry, I needed reassurance and support. If that could not be given, I was at least looking for guidance or some answers to my questions. My first meetings with my administration yielded little in terms of either. This is not being critical in any way. These people too were having difficulty coping and understanding the focus of the project and the effects it would have on their schools.

In spite of all the confusion and uncertainty I felt, I remained enthusiastic. Perhaps it was the idea of improving my teaching or sharing productive techniques with my colleagues that kept the flame of enthusiasm burning.

Over the next few months of meetings with my administration and further discussions with my colleagues, I came to the conclusion that the subject and style of my inquiry would have to be of my own choosing. The inquiry was to be specific to my classroom, my philosophy, and my questions. This project had given me the ownership to inquire about what interested me. Was it something I wanted to prove? Was it something I wanted to discover and share with the teaching world? Was it something I wished to validate? These options were all available to me. I just had to decide which of them I would focus on and in which specific area. Unfortunately for me, it was my most difficult problem and one which took me the majority of the first year to narrow down. The support I received from members of the "catalyst team" during this stage was encouraging. All of them helped me to focus my thoughts and questions and were genuinely excited about the various possibilities. However, each suggested a different inquiry which gave me more choices, the last thing I needed! Gradually my confusion and worry were becoming frustration. At this point my enthusiasm was at its lowest point. I decided to make three videotapes of my classroom, looking at a variety of situations. At least this way I would have some data to fall back on should I focus on a particular topic of interest. Believe it or not, two of these tapes did not turn out because of technological problems of one sort or another, and I had to redo them. More fuel for the fire of frustration now turned to anger.

I had written off the first year of the TALK Project by May. It was then that the project began to take on special meaning for me. I had the chance to view the tapes that I had made of my class. Looking at them, I began to notice confused faces, children unsure of expectations, groups not following directions, and above all verbose directions or presentations by the teacher — me. Regardless of what I had set out to prove, discover, or

106

validate, I had stumbled upon flaws in my teaching. I had inadvertently produced for me a reason for the project. For the two months that remained in the school year, I began to take a closer look at my teaching. I closely scrutinized my teaching methods, my talk, group discussions, my kids during group work or activity times, and my observation skills. I was now researching myself, my children, and the dynamics of my classroom, and I began looking at ways in which I could effect change to produce an environment more conducive to learning. Over those months I revised many of my programs, re-evaluated some of my units that had worked well in the past, and reviewed and restructured some aspects of my groupings within the class. Through all of this self-analysis I became more thoughtful and diligent in my efforts to improve my abilities as a classroom teacher. The opportunity to become a better practitioner by researching my own classroom was and always will be for me the most important aspect of the TALK Project.

The second most important aspect of the project for me was validation. David Booth had taken five of my children to help him create a "Booktalk" video. Through his talks with them and information he observed in the context of the video sequences which he chose, he saw some things which led him to believe that my methods of teaching in group discussions of novels were enabling my children to enjoy literature and develop their interpretive and critical comprehension skills. He asked me to analyse this further, and I continue to do so to this day. He made me aware of a variety of professional literature to read to examine the different trends in this area. I found the readings to be enlightening and educational. Although my inquiry — which was ultimately about response to literature through book talk — may seem of little importance in terms of the overall program I was teaching, it had great meaning for me and influence on many of my classroom practices. Again it provided me with a chance for further reflection, modification, and growth in my teaching skills and methods.

In short, the first year of the project was for me exciting, confusing, uncertain, enlightening, and useful, in that order. During this time of discovery, my enthusiasm reached great highs and also critical lows. My most valuable times were spent sharing ideas and discoveries with my colleagues, who came together as a support group. My discussions with the catalyst team became more meaningful as the year went on. Although I never completely focused on one specific subject, I did come up with some ideas. And I began to realize that it was we the teachers who had to take ownership of our own research and inquiries. It was then that I reached a level of comfort with the meaning of the project and its goals. I was fully aware that the project would undergo a variety of changes and I anticipated further confusing dilemmas as the project began its second year.

My responsibilities over the course of the second year were somewhat different. As acting vice-principal, I changed my focus from the individual goals I set for myself to the collective goals of the school. Instead of planning my inquiry around my interests and questions, I focused on providing an environment in which the staff could fulfil its aspirations in classroom research. Since the project was one of the school's primary interests, I became involved in planning how the project would be presented to both our new and existing members of staff. Establishing the methods by which this was done was critical to the success of the project in the school. The principal and I were fortunate enough to share similar viewpoints and opinions on the opportunities the project offered teachers. We planned to use a core group of five teachers who had been actively involved in the past year to inform our whole staff of the pitfalls they had encountered — and the potential they saw. We decided to take the first professional activity day in September to have a panel discussion about the project. This sharing session, which was an honest and fair appraisal of the project through the eyes of these five teachers, was informal and non-threatening. In my mind, professional development techniques are most effective when given by teachers to other teachers. Supported by a member of the catalyst team, who was invited to provide additional background information during the session, the professional activity day was a success. Immediately, "networking" groups started. The initial confusion and uncertainty that had troubled us the year before were not apparent. Teachers left the session with a basic understanding of what the project was about, the effects it would have on individual teachers (both positive and negative), and the opportunities it provided for professional growth and development.

As the next few weeks unfolded, the most difficult part of my role was keeping apprised of all the changes and developments that occurred. The setting up of a communication network to do so was a difficult job. I saw the responsibility of the administrator as being that of a monitor. I felt monitoring was essential for knowing when to intervene, encourage, support, assist, and guide. Reflecting on my own history in the project, I set out to smoothe the bumps in the road. Because of the individuality of the inquiries, it was important to lend my ears but to keep hands off. I did not see my job as being to take possession of inquiries and suggest changes and modifications to them. That would defeat the whole purpose of the project. I was a liaison, taking the concerns, anxieties, and frustrations of the staff and voicing them at the regular monthly meeting of the catalyst team.

The most satisfying aspect of my role as an administrator was promoting staff discoveries and encouraging teachers to share these with other schools and boards at conferences or staff meetings. The growth and emerging confidence of teachers I witnessed needed to be shared and nurtured.

Many of the administrators involved in the project felt that part of their role was to share some information about the project with parents. Although I'm not totally against the idea, I am of the belief that this sharing can take place successfully only when the objectives of the project are fully understood and the presenters (whether teachers, principals, or superintendents) have reached a level of comfort and confidence in talking about it. Parents are rarely very comfortable with any form of change or variance from the norm.

Our school has just completed its second year in the project and we are just beginning — and I stress *beginning* — to understand the project and its objectives. We have not yet shared with parents any information about the project, nor have we asked teachers to present information about it formally. Providing a merely sketchy overview and background of the project and bringing up classroom research might be enough to alarm many parents, and any sharing should be left until astute planning and an organized presentation can facilitate proper understanding.

In summarizing, I would like to outline my reflections and provide some suggestions for the future of the project. I realize that being in the unique position of both teacher and administrator during the course of the project has given me a perspective that no one else will likely have. Therefore, I stress that what follow are suggestions and suggestions only, and are not to be thought of as solutions. Every person associated with the project has or will have different views of it. This, in fact, is the beauty of it. The diversity of the scope of the project allows for a great deal of flexibility among the eight schools that are now participating in it. These are the views of one person, a result of the particular situation I found myself in.

1. Produce a "talk" publication. We have such a publication, which comes out three times a year, and is an excellent way of communicating discoveries, successes, opinions, and viewpoints. It provides teachers with a positive feeling that their inquiries are important and worth mentioning. As time has gone by, I've found that more teachers are willing to contribute and share their research. I would like to see greater input from administrators. Their views on their roles and ways in which they implement the project in their schools are important not only to other administrators but to teachers as well. The publication also provides an excellent tool for the Ministry in following the accomplishments of the project.

2. Utilize home-made resources. I think one of the primary objectives of the project is to provide a vehicle for tremendous professional growth among our teachers. Many of them have come to understand the benefits of classroom research and are at a stage when they can share this understanding with colleagues. Although efforts have been made to have these teachers talk at mini-conferences and staff meetings in other schools and boards, we have never really utilized their experiences and discoveries beyond the project itself.

3. Provide forums for sharing. This concept is more suited to the future, after the project is over. In the last year of operation the catalyst team should focus on providing opportunities for teachers to share their inquiries and findings with other teachers, through presentations at conferences or writings in educational journals. The catalyst team should try to encourage teachers to take advantage of these opportunities whenever possible. The greatest measure of the success of the project is the

number of teachers who have attained some degree of fulfilment from it.

4. Organize a method of networking. A few of the network groups that emerged in the initial stages of the project were worthwhile and fruitful for their participants. The trouble was that the groups catered to a select number of participants. If you did not have an inquiry focus that was similar to that of other participants, your contribution to the group was meaningless. I'd like to see groups or pairs of individuals with similar interests get together on a regular basis.

5. Give empowerment to teachers. One of the goals of the project was to empower individual teachers. It is a difficult item for administrators to discuss and employ; many fear and avoid it. But empowerment should not be viewed merely on an individual basis. As Larry Lezotte says, "the whole of the staff should be empowered to use their collective knowledge to make collective judgments and take collective actions towards school improvement". If one thinks of the TALK Project as a means to school improvement, then empowerment must be given to all the teachers involved in the process of inquiry. Together with their staffs, administrators should facilitate opportunities to collectively plan and set objectives for the project's implementation within the school itself. In addition, the administration should actively support each staff member's discoveries and opinions and look for ways in which these can be shared.

6. Become involved by conducting an inquiry of your own. To fully understand the whole process of the project, I firmly believe you have to experience it yourself before you can begin to share opinions and feelings about it. Researching an inquiry of his or her own will give an administrator a first-hand look at the benefits and dilemmas inquiries offer, as well as serving as an example to the staff. Any staff will take you much more seriously in your discussions with them if you yourself have pursued an inquiry. The whole situation reminds me of the analogy of promoting reading in the classroom. If the teacher chooses not to read during silent reading time, how can he or she expect the students to be enthused about it?

7. Allow for freedom of voice. Administrators should attempt where possible to give their staffs every opportunity to express themselves liberally about the project and its methods or the goals and objectives that have been set for their schools. Creating an environment in which staff are permitted to speak freely without fear of repercussions should be an essential component of each administrator's goals. This enables the administrator to acquire a realistic understanding of the situation within the school rather than the superficial one which he or she often has. Finding out the true picture will assist the principal/vice-principal in effecting positive change within the school and also within the scope of the project at steering committee meetings.

8. Continue to meet as a group. Last year the principals and vice-principals began meeting on a regular basis to discuss issues that arose from the project. This was a worthwhile venture and allowed a great many concerns and ideas to be shared. The only change I'd like to see here is that each meeting should have a definitive focus (e.g., implementation ideas, collective goal-making, possible models, etc.).

I also have suggestions for teachers themselves. Since my belief is that the strength of any project like this lies with them, they must make a concerted effort. Our system is blessed with many fine professionals who do justice to our profession. It is with this in mind that I make the following suggestions.

9. Accept and welcome positive change. If the TALK Project has one outstanding feature, it is that it has provided teachers with an opportunity to take a close, in-depth look at a facet or facets of their programs and change or modify them so that children learn better. It has also enabled teachers to share their findings with colleagues. Educational methods have undergone changes throughout history, and just as education changes, we as professional educators need to add to what we know so that we can improve methods ourselves. We must constantly look at our own programs and investigate and improve the methods and practices we employ. In addition to this, we must be willing to share successes with our colleagues at every opportunity. Good teaching is a condition of the mind. The project gave many teachers an awareness of the benefits of classroom research.

We must continue to employ this awareness in our future careers, long after the Ministry has withdrawn its funding for the TALK Project.

10. Continue to pursue opportunities to share with colleagues. We as educators have a responsibility to our colleagues to share with them our discoveries and opinions. Continued presentations at conferences and publishing articles in educational journals should be encouraged and supported. Teachers should also be willing to enter into a network or partnership model for meaningful professional dialogue and for promoting staff or professional development.

In conclusion, I see the primary benefit of the TALK Project as being professional development. The growth a teacher or group of teachers can make over the course of a year is remarkable. Involvement in a project such as this can lead to more innovative programming, increased professional reading, a self-analysis of teaching ability, and sharing with colleagues on an informal (networking) or more formal basis (conferences, presentations to other staff members, professional articles).

For me the whole experience in this project has led to professional growth. I am saddened at the thought of moving to a school that is not involved in it. I hope that the catalyst team will investigate ways that teachers leaving the project schools can remain involved somehow. If this is impossible, I will at least take with me some new ideas and a new-found state of mind — that of what Nancie Atwell calls the "thoughtful practicioner".

Bibliography

These resources were made available to the teachers in the schools that participated in the TALK Project.

Adelman, Clem. *Uttering, Muttering*. London: Grant McIntyre Ltd., 1981.

Bailey, Charles, and David Bridges. *Mixed Ability Grouping: A Philosophical Perspective. Introductory Studies in Philosophy of Education*. Philip Snelders and Colin Wringe, eds. London: George Allen & Unwin, 1983.

Barnes, Douglas. *From Communication to Curriculum*. New York: Penguin, 1976.

Barnes, Douglas, James Britton, and Mike Torbe. *Language, the Learner and the School*. 4th ed. New York: Penguin, 1986.

Barrs, Myra, et al. *The Primary Language Record Handbook for Teachers*. London: ILEA Centre for Language in Primary Education, 1989. (Markham, Ont.: Pembroke; Portsmouth, NH: Heinemann.)

Barton, Bob. *Tell Me Another: Storytelling and Reading Aloud at Home, at School and in the Community*. Markham, Ont.: Pembroke, 1986. (Portsmouth, NH: Heinemann.)

Barton, Bob, and David Booth. *Stories in the Classroom*. Markham, Ont.: Pembroke, 1990. (Portsmouth, NH: Heinemann.)

Beveridge, Michael. *Children Thinking through Language*. London: Edward Arnold, 1982.

Brissendon, Tom. *Talking about Mathematics*. London: Basil Blackwell, 1988.

Britton, James. *Language and Learning*. London: Penguin, 1976.

Buber, Martin. *I and Thou*. New York: Charles Scribner's Sons, 1958.

Burgess, Anthony. *Language Made Plain*. London: Fontana, 1984.

Chambers, Aidan. *Booktalk: Occasional Writing on Literature and Children*. London: Bodley Head, 1985.

Creber, J.W. Patrick. *Lost for Words — Language and Education Failure*. London: Penguin, 1972.

Davies, Alan. *Language and Learning in Home and School*. Portsmouth, NH: Heinemann, 1982.

DeVilliers, Peter A. and Jill G. *Early Language — The Developing Child*. Cambridge, Mass: Harvard University Press, 1982.

Donaldson, Margaret. *Children's Minds*. London: Fontana, 1978.

Dunn, Sonja. *Butterscotch Dreams: Chants for Fun and Learning*. Markham, Ont.: Pembroke, 1988. (Portsmouth, NH: Heinemann.)

_____. *Crackers and Crumbs*. Markham, Ont.: Pembroke, 1990. (Portsmouth, NH: Heinemann)

Enright, D. Scott, and Mary Lou McCloskey. *Integrating English*. New York: Addison-Wesley, 1988.

Fleishman, Paul. *Joyful Noise*. New York: Harper and Row, 1988.

Fry, Donald. "Children Talk about Books: Seeing Themselves as Readers". *English, Language, and Education*. Anthony Adams, ed. Milton Keynes, UK: Open University Press, 1985.

Gahagan, D.M. and G.A. *Talk Reform*. London: Routledge & Kegan Paul, 1972.

Garvey, Catherine. *Children's Talk*. London: Fontana, 1984.

Greene, Judith. *Thinking and Language*. London: Methuen, 1982.

Hayhoe, Mike, and Stephen Parker. *Working with Fiction*. Sydney Hill and Colin Reid, eds. London: Edward Arnold, 1984.

Heath, Shirley Brice. *Ways with Words: Language, Life, and Work in Communities and Classrooms*. Cambridge: Cambridge University Press, 1983.

Johnson, David W., and Frank P. Johnson. *Joining Together — Group Theory and Group Skills*. Englewood Cliffs, NJ: Prentice-Hall, 1987.

Johnson, David W., and Roger T. Johnson. *Circles of Learning — Cooperation in the Classroom*. Alexandria, VA: ASCD, 1984.

Knowles, Lewis. *Encouraging Talk*. London: Methuen, 1983.

Lightfoot, Martin, and Nancy Martin. *The Word for Teaching is Learning: Essays for James Britton*. Portsmouth, NH: Heinemann, 1988.

Maclure, Margaret, Terry Phillips, and Andrew Wilkinson, eds. *Oracy Matters*. Milton Keynes, UK: Open University Press, 1988.

Medway, Peter. *Finding a Language — Autonomy and Learning in School.* London: Writers and Readers Publishing Co-operative, 1980.

Mills, Richard W. *Observing Children in the Primary Classroom.* London: Unwin Hyman Ltd., 1988.

Moore, Bill, and David Booth. *Poems Please.* Markham, Ont.: Pembroke, 1989.

Moyle, Donald. *Children's Words.* London: Grant McIntyre Ltd., 1982.

Opie, Iona and Peter. *The Lore and Language of Schoolchildren.* Oxford: Oxford University Press, 1976.

Osborne, Roger, and Peter Freyberg. *Learning in Science.* Portsmouth, NH: Heinemann, 1985.

Paley, Vivian G. *Wally's Stories: Conversations in the Kindergarten.* Cambridge, Mass.: Harvard University Press, 1985.

Peterson, Ralph, and Maryann Eads. *Grand Conversations.* Toronto: Scholastic, 1988.

Phelan, Patricia, ed. *Talking to Learn: Classroom Practices in Teaching English.* Urbana, Ill: NCTE, 1989.

Pinnell, Gay Su. *Discovering Language with Children.* Urbana, Ill: NCTE, 1980.

Robinson, W.P. *Language and Social Behaviour.* London: Penguin, 1972.

Rosen, Michael. *Did I Hear You Write?* Richmond Hill, Ont.: Scholastic, 1989.

Smith, E. Brooks, Kenneth S. Goodman, and Robert Meredith. *Language and Thinking in School.* New York: Holt, Reinhart & Winston, 1976.

Squire, James R. *The Dynamics of Language Learning.* Urbana, Ill: ERIC Clearinghouse on Reading and Communication Skills, 1987.

Swartz, Larry. *Dramathemes.* Markham, Ont.: Pembroke, 1988. (Portsmouth, NH: Heinemann.)

Tough, Jan. *The Development of Meaning.* London: George Allen & Unwin, 1977.

_____. *Talk for Teaching and Learning.* London: Ward Lock Education, 1981.

Watson, Dorothy, Carolyn Burke, and Jerome Harste. *Whole Language: Inquiring Voices.* Richmond Hill, Ont.: Scholastic, 1989.

Wells, Gordon. *Language Development in the Pre-school Years.* Cambridge: Cambridge University Press, 1985.

_____. *The Meaning Makers: Children Learning Language and Using Language to Learn.* Toronto: Unwin, 1986.

Wells, Judith. *Children's Language and Learning.* Englewood Cliffs, NJ: Prentice-Hall, 1980.

White, Connie. *Jevon Doesn't Sit at the Back Anymore.* Richmond Hill, Ont.: Scholastic, 1990.

Wilkinson, Andrew. *The Foundations of Language — Talking and Reading in Young Children.* Oxford: Oxford University Press, 1971.

_____. *Language and Education.* Oxford: Oxford University Press, 1975.

Wood, Barbara Sundene. *Development of Functional Communication Competencies: Grades 7-12.* Urbana, Ill.: ERIC Clearinghouse on Reading and Communication Skills, 1977.

Yardley, Alice. *Exploration and Language.* London: Evans Brothers, 1974.